7 MEASURES OF SUCCESS

What Remarkable Associations Do That Others Don't

The Center for Association Leadership

WASHINGTON, DC

Information in this book is accurate as of the time of publication and consistent with standards of good practice in the general management community. As research and practice advance, however, standards may change. For this reason it is recommended that readers evaluate the applicability of any recommendations in light of particular situations and changing standards.

ASAE: The Center for Association Leadership
1575 I Street, NW
Washington, DC 20005-1103
Phone: (202) 626-2723; (888) 950-2723 outside the metropolitan Washington, DC area
Fax: (202) 220-6439
Email: books@asaecenter.org
We connect great ideas and great people to inspire leadership and achievement in the association community.

Keith C. Skillman, CAE, Vice President, Publications, ASAE: The Center for Association Leadership
Baron Williams, CAE, Director of Book Publishing, ASAE: The Center for Association Leadership
Cover by Beth Lower, Art Director, ASAE: The Center for Association Leadership
Interior by Troy Scott Parker, CimarronDesign.com

This book is available at a special discount when ordered in bulk quantities. For information, contact the ASAE Member Service Center at (202) 371-0940.

A complete catalog of titles is available on the ASAE website at www.asaecenter.org.

Published by Association Management Press.

ISBN-13: 978-0-88034-341-1
ISBN-10: 0-88034-341-9

Printed in the United States of America.

10 9 8 7 6 5 4 3 2 1

With thanks and appreciation to

Jim Collins, our mentor,

who graciously and generously shared his knowledge,

provided invaluable insights,

and inspired us throughout this research project.

Contents

Foreword

By Jim Collins

Best-selling author of *Good to Great* and *Built to Last*

A SSOCIATIONS ARE the hidden glue of our society and economy. Like the mortar that holds the bricks of a building in place, associations go largely unnoticed, yet they do much to hold the entire structure together. As such, associations cannot settle for being only good; they must work toward greatness. But what separates exceptional associations from good ones? What does it take to turn an association from good to great, and how can excellence be sustained?

In 2002, ASAE & The Center for Association Leadership assembled a team of association leaders into an ambitious multiyear effort to address exactly these questions. "If you're serious about understanding what makes for great associations," I urged, "someone in the association world should undertake a matched-pair study."

One of my mentors, Jerry Porras, conceived of the historical matched-pair method at Stanford University in the late 1980s, when we were working as research colleagues puzzling over a vexing question. If you look over 100 years of history, most well run companies adopt most of the same basic practices, and yet few become great. It doesn't matter whether you are looking at the principles of scientific management, statistical quality control, management by objectives,

Six Sigma, decentralization, reengineering, or strategic planning; the best practices tend to spread across all major companies.

Yet some companies become truly great, while others do not. The obvious question is: Why? If most companies eventually adopt largely the same practices, then what enduring principles do in fact distinguish those that become great from those that do not?

Research that examines only successful outcomes contains a fundamental flaw, what Porras called the "discover buildings trap." If you study highly successful public corporations, you'll see that they all occupy buildings, but you would equally see that 100 percent of mediocre performers also occupy buildings. The critical question is not what successful organizations share in common but what *distinguishes* great organizations from their less-successful counterparts.

In response to this dilemma, Porras had a significant research insight: Apply the idea of "twin studies" to social systems, not just in a snapshot, but over time. (In a genetic twin study, you examine the life trajectories of twins separated at birth to glean insight into nature versus nurture.) Most industries give us at least one pair of twins—two companies born in the same era, with the same market opportunities, facing the same demographics, technology shifts, and socioeconomic trends. But when you fast-forward the tape of history, some companies become great while their twin brothers and sisters do not.

Consider General Electric (GE) and Westinghouse. Both companies came into existence near the start of the 20th century. Both had access to capital and faced a gigantic opportunity to disseminate electrical power. Yet, by the end of the 20th century, GE and Westinghouse had become very different companies. GE became an icon of excellence; Westinghouse, while a successful company, failed to attain the same stature. Porras' idea was to study rigorously selected industrial twins (matched pairs) over a long enough period of time to separate short-term variables—such as luck, a single charismatic leader, or a great idea—from timeless principles that distinguish exceptional organizations from merely good ones.

Porras' methodological insight guided our six-year research effort that led to the book *Built to Last* and inspired the method behind the five-year effort that led to *Good to Great*.

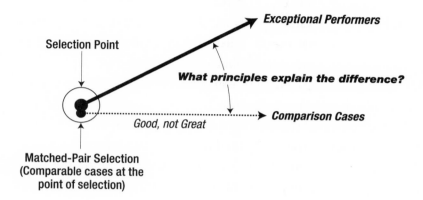

Shortly after we published *Good to Great*, I had dinner with Morten Hansen, a former member of the research team who had become a professor at Harvard. He stumped me with this question: "What is the most significant idea to come from the research so far?"

I thought about it for a minute and then offered two possibilities: Level 5 Leadership—leaders who display a paradoxical blend of personal humility and professional will—and Preserve the Core/ Stimulate Progress—the discipline to hold core values and mission constant while endlessly adapting operating practices and strategies to a changing world.

"No, I don't think so," pushed Hansen. "Try again."

I mentioned a couple of other concepts from our work and he again said, "No, I don't think so."

"What do you think?" I finally asked.

"The research method itself," he said. "It could be applied to any sector of society and to almost any social question."

Inspired by Hansen's observation, we began to challenge leaders throughout the social sectors that they could—indeed, *should*—do matched-pair analyses, to answer their own questions: What systematically separates great schools, hospitals, universities, police departments, associations, orchestras, or any other set of entities from merely good ones?

But we encountered a problem. This type of research requires at least three times more effort than studying highly successful organizations by themselves. Many social sector leaders expressed interest, but most backed away when they realized that this research requires not months but *years* of effort.

Not so for ASAE which, to my knowledge, became the first group to take on the challenge of applying our research method to a social sector question. During a four-year period (2002–2006), the ASAE team persisted with the research project, an effort made all the more remarkable by the fact that most team members volunteered.

The team made four trips to my office in Boulder, Colorado, to discuss research progress. My own involvement in the study was limited to serving as an informal mentor, giving the research team pointers the way a faculty advisor might guide a particularly dedicated doctoral student working on a thesis. And, like a thesis advisor, the professor can take no credit for the work of the student. The team put in the thousands of hours and gave up time away from their work and families. The team selected the study set, gathered the data, sifted the evidence, and drew the conclusions. Credit for this work goes entirely to them.

The power of the research lies not just in what the team found but equally in what it did *not* find. I've always enjoyed the Sherlock Holmes story *The Adventure of Silver Blaze*, wherein Holmes cracked the case with the "curious incident of the dog in the night-time." But the dog did nothing in the night-time! Ah, *that* was the curious incident—the fact that the dog did not bark—which led Holmes to the conclusion that the criminal must have been someone who knew the dog well.

In matched-pair analysis, the "dogs that do not bark" provide as much insight as positive discovery. Board size did not bark in this study. Democratic board selection did not bark. Outside professional management did not bark. The distinction between staff-driven versus member-driven did not bark; what matters is being obsessively *data*-driven, combined with the creativity and discipline to act on that data in ways that meet your members' needs better than any other organization.

Disciplined people who engage in disciplined thought and who take disciplined action—this simple mantra captures much of what separates any great institution from the average. In this report, the ASAE research team shines a light on the disciplines peculiar to associations. But even more important, the team issues a challenge. For implicit within the matched-pair method we find a central truth: Some organizations perform better than others, despite facing comparable opportunities and circumstances.

Every association can deliver better results for its members. The research team has done the community of associations a tremendous service by undertaking this research. Now it is up to you to make your association better tomorrow than it is today, better the next day than tomorrow, every single day, forever.

– Jim Collins
  Boulder, Colorado
  June 10, 2006

Preface to the Revised Edition

Since the Measures of Success Task Force completed its work in 2006, the external environment in which associations operate has changed considerably. The near-collapse of the U.S. financial and housing markets, coupled with a prolonged recession, have challenged associations to maintain fiscal stability and continually demonstrate value in a world fraught with economic uncertainty.

Given these pressures, it seemed like a good time to check back with the nine organizations that had exhibited seven distinguishing characteristics, or measures, and thus earned the "remarkable association" designation. How had they weathered the recession and addressed its lingering effects? Were they doing anything differently? Did the seven measures still resonate with their staff members and volunteer leaders?

To find out, we reconnected with the nine remarkable associations through in-depth interviews, either with the CEOs or senior staff, and reviews of association materials and resources. Reconnecting did not require the whole Measures of Success Task force to reconvene, but we relied on one of the original members to conduct follow-up interviews and integrate the resulting updates into this revised edition. Since the publication of the original book, there have been hundreds of meetings, courses, workshops, lectures, and discussion groups that have discussed the book's findings and how to incorporate them into one's own association. This edition has also been restructured slightly, as well as expanded significantly with the addition of a new chapter. In Chapter 6: Putting the 7 Measures to Work, you'll find the stories of three associations that decided to incorporate the seven measures into their cultures and operations.

Without question, the updating process confirmed the integrity of the original research. The seven measures remain as relevant today as when the Measures of Success Task Force first identified them. It's important to remember that, in most instances, the associations exhibiting these characteristics had experienced at least one severe crisis—whether related to finances, leadership, or membership—during the 15 years examined in the the original research period and had recovered well. In other words, the seven measures of success were not forged only during times of growth, expansion, or plenty. Given remarkable associations' proven ability to thrive, even in less-than-ideal circumstances, it's not surprising that they emerged in solid financial shape from the economic meltdown of 2008.

To be sure, the recession affected these associations, leading in some instances to decreased membership, budget and program cut-backs, and salary freezes. Along the way, association leaders and staff had to make some difficult choices. But thanks to their disciplined adherence to a set of core principles and practices—reflected in this book as the seven measures—these associations all had a culture in place that enabled them to effectively address different economic realities, even if the industry or profession they represent had taken a big hit during the recession.

Since the first printing of this book, the associations in the study group kept busy streamlining their mission statements and goals, revising programs and services—often to reflect the growing pop-ularity of mobile applications and social media—encouraging conversations about what their members wanted and needed most, and searching out new alliance partners to make resources stretch even further. They also demonstrated the will to act, as observed in the original research. One association, for example, introduced a massive restructuring of its governance structure; another restructured its staff to focus on gathering more detailed data to support its business decisions. And these adaptable associations did it all with a minimum of hand-wringing and second-guessing. Even in the face of unprecedented economic pressures, they stayed true to their core and developed contingency plans—and then took action. In short, the remarkable associations continued exhibiting the behavior that made them exemplary in the first place.

Joe McGuire, CAE
Chairman-Elect, ASAE
Chairman, ASAE Foundation
President, Association of Home Appliance Manufacturers

Susan Robertson, CAE
President, ASAE Foundation
Executive Vice-President, ASAE

February 2012

Editor's note: When *7 Measures of Success* was first released in 2006, the two organizations involved were referred to as ASAE & The Center for Association Leadership. Since then, both organizations have adopted new names. ASAE: The Center for Association Leadership, or ASAE for short, is the 501(c)(6) representing more than 21,000 association executives and industry partners. The ASAE Foundation, formerly The Center for Association Leadership, is a 501(c)(3) organization dedicated to advancing association and nonprofit leadership with the support of generous individual and corporate contributions.

Preface to the First Edition

AM I running my association in the best possible way?
You, like many other association executives, probably grapple with that question at least once a day, if not once an hour. We're always looking for the product, the strategy, the approach that makes our organizations more efficient, more effective and, above all, more successful.

Over the years, countless books, magazine articles, journals, meetings, conference sessions, and other resources have contributed to the building of an impressive store of knowledge related to association management. In fact, the profession itself has outlined that body of knowledge and developed a certification exam to assess whether someone demonstrates it.

Much of what we know about association management, however, is not based on empirical data. Rather, it is based on common sense, as well as individual and collective experience. This anecdotal information has given rise to numerous, oft-repeated "conventional wisdoms" about our profession that may—or may not—stand up under scientific scrutiny.

A Useful Model

In 1994, Jim Collins gained national attention with the publication of *Built to Last*. Co-authored by Jerry Porras, the book addressed one basic question: What makes the truly exceptional companies *different* from other companies?

After identifying highly visionary companies through a jurying process, Collins and Porras matched each one to a control organization. For example, American Express, a visionary company, was matched with Wells Fargo. Then, for each pair, they carefully examined a massive amount of information about each company. In the process, they identified basic concepts or successful habits that set the visionary companies apart from others.

Ever the curious researcher, Collins reflected on the fact that the visionary companies profiled in *Built to Last* had always been great. So what factors would transform a good company into a great one? A desire to answer that compelling question prompted Collins' next book, *Good to Great*. In it, he employed a methodology similar to what he and Porras had used before, including matched research pairs. For each great company, he selected a counterpart in the same industry that had had the same opportunities and similar resources but had failed to make the long-term transition from good to great.

Several of the findings reported in *Good to Great*, such as the need to focus on the core mission, resonated with the association community. Others were more problematic. For example, Collins found that great organizations "get the right people on the bus." But most associations and nonprofit organizations have a shared management responsibility between staff and volunteers; no one individual within an association has the same latitude as a corporate CEO to get people on or off the team.

Early in 2002, several members of The Center for Association Leadership's Research Committee heard Collins speak at a conference called Digital Now in Orlando, Florida. They agreed that, while not all of the results applied to associations, the methodology used in *Good to Great* certainly had value. Even better, Collins enthusiastically supported the idea that the methodology he had used could help identify what made outstanding associations different from others.

Teaming Up

Thanks to the efforts of Hugh Lee of Fusion Productions, several committee members had the opportunity to meet with Collins at his office in Boulder, Colorado. The office is a converted school building—in fact, the conference room occupies a portion of Collins' old first-grade classroom.

In his first-grade report card, which is framed and hanging on the wall, Collins' teacher had noted, "Jimmy is a nice boy and plays well with others"—a trait that he has never lost. Greeting us with warmth and enthusiasm, Jim quickly put us at ease. Within minutes, we were knee-deep in a discussion of an association research project.

From the outset, Collins agreed to mentor us through the research process. He was interested in seeing others replicate his work in their own environments, while we were interested in finding our own answers. Thus began our partnership. Much like a professor providing guidance to doctoral students, Collins would serve as our advisor. He would ensure we remained true to his research methodology and provide a structure for us to follow, along with advice when needed. The actual work, however—from start to finish—would be our own.

Willingness to Share

The Measures of Success Project, as it came to be known, was the first internal research project undertaken completely by The Center for Association Leadership. It involved many years of staff time, countless hours of volunteer time, and several moments of spirited discussion and debate.

This research project would not have come to fruition, however, without the participation of the associations profiled in the pages of this book. Those that served as our research "study group" are clearly identified. As truly exceptional organizations, they rose above the rest in many ways.

Keep in mind, however, that the associations paired with the study group for comparison purposes are also strong performers. They simply did not rise to the same level of greatness during the 15 years prior to and including 2003 that we choose as the focus of this study. We were looking for the qualities or factors that explained the differences between the two groups—or, as Collins would say, what made one association a gold-medal winner and what made its comparison organization a silver- or bronze-medal winner.

In some cases, as with Olympic performances when only a second or two may separate the winners of the gold and silver medals, the difference was not that great. In fact, had the time period being studied been slightly different, several associations in the comparison group may well have been contenders for the study group. To keep attention focused on the aggregate results, we decided not to publicly identify the organizations that served as the comparison half of the matched pairs.

Agreeing to participate in the study was no small commitment for organizations in either research group. While Collins relied on public documents for much of his work, we had to ask the participating organizations to gather and supply membership and financial data, not to mention information about leadership, staffing, operations, governance, culture, products, and markets. Researchers and task force members also conducted on-site interviews that required a considerable time commitment from the organizations visited.

Because associations in both the study and comparison groups opened their doors and their books to the task force, we had the opportunity to see what the differences are. Some differences are subtle; others are dramatic. All offer considerable food for thought.

At one point during the research process, when the end was not yet in sight, Collins provided this reassurance: "Do your work right, and it will be timeless." If we have achieved that goal, it is because he was our mentor, our guide, and, at times, our cheerleader.

Through his work, Collins clearly demonstrated that, through careful study and analysis, one could discover what made great companies different from good ones. We hope we have done the same for associations and, in the process, contributed to the advancement of our profession.

Michael E. Gallery, Ph.D., CAE
President, OPIS, LLC, and Chair, Measures of Success
Task Force (2002–2006)

Susan Sarfati, CAE
President and Chief Executive Officer, The Center for Association Leadership, and Executive Vice President, American Society of Association Executives

August 2006

CHAPTER I

A Study of Differences

TEMPTING THOUGH it may be, you can't write an equation for success in an association. Too many factors come into play: developments in the industry or profession, the economy, the leadership style of staff and volunteers, and the needs of the members themselves, to name just a few. Even if one association achieves success by doing A, B, and C, there's no guarantee that another association, following the same equation, will enjoy the same result.

That said, some factors undoubtedly show up more frequently than others among successful associations. These organizations are highly efficient as well as highly effective. They not only provide products and services of value to their members but also do so at the right time, in the right way, and at the right cost. In short, they know what needs to be done, and they do it well.

But what factors truly set successful associations apart from others? What unique characteristics do they, as a group, share that makes them *different* from other associations? Those are the questions at the heart of the long-term research project undertaken by The Center for Association Leadership, which culminates in this book.

Setting the Stage

Conducting rigorous, objective research about what makes remarkable associations is challenging, a fact that may contribute to the scarcity of such research in the association world.

Much of what we know about association management is based on anecdotal evidence, personal experience, common sense, and research from business and other sectors. There are obvious limitations in relying solely on these sources of information. First, the information gleaned from these sources often applies to particular situations. Generalizing from one situation to another can be problematic; an approach that works for one association may be a failure for another group. You risk investing your association's scarce resources—including time, money, attention, and effort—in popular solutions that sound good but make no difference in the long run.

Objective research is one of the most effective ways to learn which behaviors, actions, and attitudes have strategic impact on an organization and its success. That was the rationale for the general approach and methodology used by the Measures of Success Task Force of The Center for Association Leadership as it attempted to discover what constitutes success in a voluntary association.

From the beginning, the task force carefully reviewed and embraced the rigorous research underpinning the books *Built to Last* and *Good to Great.* Jim Collins and Jerry Porras understood the essential yet intangible relationship among core beliefs and practices and an organization's soul. As mission-driven organizations, associations depend on such beliefs and practices.

What makes the truly exceptional companies similar to one another, and what differentiates them from other companies? This question became the basis of *Built to Last.* Collins and Porras set out to learn about the visionary company, one that succeeds across generations, changes in leadership, and product lifecycles. *Built to Last,* the product of this research, focuses on industrial titans such as Boeing, IBM, Sony, Procter & Gamble, and Merck, all founded before 1950.

Of the 36 companies Collins and Porras studied, 18 were considered visionaries, while another 18 formed a comparison group. They compared each of the 18 truly exceptional companies—as measured by longevity, consistently strong performance, and superior financial results—with a prominent and successful, but less remarkable, competitor.

Collins and Porras found that organizations with vision have a much higher likelihood of enduring success. Defining vision as a global statement of *who we are* and *where we are headed,* the authors identified four key elements of vision: core ideology; core purpose; big, hairy, audacious goals (highly ambitious goals that reflect the vision); and a vivid description of the goal. In *Built to Last,* the authors also challenge much conventional wisdom propounded by venerable schools of business, pundits, and the like.

In his next book, *Good to Great,* Collins focused on companies that had started out good and had transformed themselves into great companies. What, he wondered, had they done to distinguish themselves from those that remained good?

For the research that led to *Good to Great,* Collins required an objective measure. Accordingly, the research team analyzed the stock performance of Fortune 500 companies. Among these, they identified 11 companies that had first achieved and then maintained dramatic increases in their stock price(s) while other companies in their industries had maintained good, but not spectacular, increases in stock price.

For each great company, Collins selected a counterpart company in the same industry, one that had experienced the same opportunities and had similar resources but had not transformed itself from good to great. These counterpart companies formed the comparison group.

Together, *Built to Last* and *Good to Great* identified a framework of concepts that correlate with great companies in contrast to merely good ones. Those concepts are:

Level 5 Leadership. Level 5 leaders are ambitious first and foremost about the cause, the organization, the work—not themselves—and they have the fierce resolve to do whatever it takes to fulfill that ambition. A Level 5 leader displays a paradoxical blend of personal humility and professional will.

First Who, Then What. Those who build great organizations make sure they have the right people on the bus, the wrong people off the bus, and the right people in the key seats before they figure out where to drive the bus. They always think first about who and then about what.

Confront the Brutal Facts (The Stockdale Paradox). Retain unwavering faith that you can and will prevail in the end, regardless of the difficulties, and at the same time have the discipline to confront the most brutal facts of the current reality.

Hedgehog Concept. Greatness comes about by a series of good decisions consistent with a simple, coherent concept. This hedgehog is an operating model that reflects understanding of three intersecting circles: what you can be the best in world at, what you are deeply passionate about, and what best drives your economic or resource engine.

Culture of Discipline. Disciplined people who engage in disciplined thought and take disciplined action, operating with freedom within a framework of responsibilities, are the cornerstone of a culture that creates greatness. In a culture of discipline, people do not have jobs; they have responsibilities.

The Flywheel. In building greatness, there is no single defining action, no grand program, no one killer innovation, no solitary lucky break, no miracle moment. Rather, the process resembles relentlessly pushing a giant, heavy flywheel in one direction, turn upon turn, building momentum until a point of breakthrough, and beyond.

Clock Building, Not Time Telling. Truly great organizations prosper through multiple generations of leaders—the exact opposite of being built around a single great leader, great idea, or specific program. Leaders in great organizations build catalytic mechanisms to stimulate progress and do not depend on having a charismatic personality to get things done; indeed, many had a "charisma bypass."

Preserve the Core/Stimulate Progress. Enduring great organizations are characterized by a fundamental duality. On one hand, they have a set of timeless core values and a core reason for being that remain constant over long periods of time. On the other hand, they have a relentless drive for change and progress, a creative compulsion that often manifests in BHAGs (Big Hairy Audacious Goals). Great organizations keep clear the difference between their core values, which never change, and operating strategies and cultural practices, which endlessly adapt to a changing world.

In the work of Collins, the Measures of Success Task Force found not only a methodology that made sense from a research standpoint but also well-defined concepts that begged to be tested in the association environment. For nearly four years, staff and volunteers gathered and reviewed data, conducted interviews and site visits, and tested hypotheses using matched pairs of associations—nine in the study group and nine in the comparison group. (See Appendix C for detailed descriptions of the methodology, timeline, and tools used by the Measures of Success Task Force.)

Ultimately, the study group comprised these nine organizations:

- AARP
- American College of Cardiology
- American Dental Association
- Associated General Contractors of America

- Girl Scouts of the USA
- National Association of Counties
- Ohio Society of Certified Public Accountants
- Radiological Society of North America
- Society for Human Resource Management

THE 7 MEASURES OF SUCCESS

Commitment to Purpose
1. A Customer Service Culture
2. Alignment of Products and Services with Mission

Commitment to Analysis and Feedback
3. Data-Driven Strategies
4. Dialogue and Engagement
5. CEO as a Broker of Ideas

Commitment to Action
6. Organizational Adaptability
7. Alliance Building

The Commitments

Eventually, the years of data gathering and analysis culminated in the identification of seven factors, or measures of success, that differentiated the remarkable associations in the study group from their counterparts in the control group. These characteristics are deeply ingrained in the study group's organizational DNA. They represent commitments consistently honored by each organization—not just intentions, aspirations, or marketing messages. (See Appendix A for profiles of the nine organizations in the study group.)

In the following chapters, you'll find detailed explanations and examples of the seven measures. No one measure outweighs the others; all contribute equally to an association's ability to innovate, grow, and thrive over time. They are not presented in any particular order or priority but rather are grouped into three categories of commitment.

Each association in the study group exemplified these seven measures of success.

Commitment to Purpose

- *A Customer Service Culture*—A "we're here to serve you" approach not only permeates all individual encounters with members but also is built into organizational structure and processes.

- *Alignment of Products and Services with Mission*—The depth and breadth of offerings are consistent with the organization's mission, which remains central and unchanging even in the midst of changes in the external environment.

Commitment to Analysis and Feedback

- *Data-Driven Strategies*—Remarkable associations have developed an expertise in gathering information as well as processes for sharing and analyzing the data to deduce what actions the data point to taking.

- *Dialogue and Engagement*—An internal conversation continually occurs among staff and volunteers about the organization's direction and priorities.

- *CEO as a Broker of Ideas*—Although the CEO may be visionary, what's more important is that the CEO facilitates visionary thinking throughout the organization.

Commitment to Action

- *Organizational Adaptability*—Remarkable associations learn from and respond to change; although willing to change, they also know what *not* to change.

- *Alliance Building*—Associations that are secure and confident in their own right seek partners and projects that complement their mission and purpose.

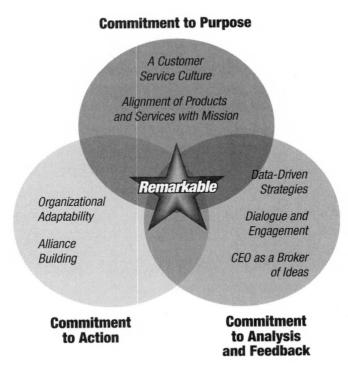

Commitment to Purpose

A Customer
Service Culture

Alignment of Products
and Services with Mission

Remarkable

Data-Driven
Strategies

Organizational
Adaptability

Dialogue and
Engagement

Alliance
Building

CEO as a Broker
of Ideas

**Commitment
to Action**

**Commitment
to Analysis
and Feedback**

Just a Sample

Please keep in mind that the nine associations in the study group simply represent a sample of exemplary associations. They are not the only nine associations that know how to achieve stellar success, nor are they the only ones that deserve to be labeled as "great" or "remarkable." No doubt other associations have registered equal or greater success in their ability to serve members and maintain a healthy financial status.

As a group, the nine study associations provide a glimpse into the world of greatness and offer seven points of entry. These seven measures of success are not intended to provide an equation for every association to follow to the letter. In fact, although all associations within the study group exhibit the seven factors, each one does so in a unique way. For example, the Radiological Society of North America and the Girl Scouts of the USA look and operate differently on the surface. But internally, both organizations have made the same commitments to purpose, analysis and feedback, and action.

The seven factors *are* intended to provide guidance, and perhaps inspiration, for both staff and volunteers who have a desire to improve their association's performance and register even greater success.

◆ ◆ ◆ ◆ ◆ ◆ ◆

Please keep in mind that the nine associations in the study group simply represent a sample of exemplary associations. They are not the only nine associations that know how to achieve stellar success.

CHAPTER 2

Commitment to Purpose

*Commitment to Purpose:
Consistently exhibiting a customer service
culture and an alignment of products and
services with organizational mission.*

How do you measure success?

When asked that question, the CEO of one association in the study group responded, "We measure success by how relevant we are to members: Are we meeting their needs? Are we anticipating their needs?"

That member-oriented mindset and focus clearly emerged from the study group. In how they are organized and operate, the study associations always focus first on what they can do for members, by anticipating and meeting member needs.

Here's how one staff member at an association in the study group articulated this commitment: "We always put the member front and center of everything we do, to ensure we are serving the mission for both individual members and the overall profession."

An Association of the Members, by the Members, for the Members

Measure 1: A Customer Service Culture

Ask employees of any association why the association exists and most will likely say, "We're here to serve our members." It's a predictable, safe response—and, in the case of remarkable associations, it also happens to be true.

Remarkable associations do not pay lip service to the idea of serving their members. On the contrary, they demonstrate their commitment to members in everything they do, from answering the phone, to responding to email, to developing quality products and services. "This would be a great place to work if it weren't for the members" is the type of humorous comment often voiced by association staff. Such statements, even in jest, are never even whispered in remarkable associations.

This first measure, having a customer service culture, goes well beyond individual encounters with members. Remarkable associations build their structures, processes, and interactions—their

SERVICE: EVERYONE'S RESPONSIBILITY

To underscore its central belief that providing excellent service to members is the responsibility of every employee, the American Dental Association (ADA) provides customer service training to all staff. In support of its overall purpose, the association also has articulated a mission and five values specifically for its employees. Here's how they read:

Mission

ADA staff are dedicated partners contributing their knowledge, experience, and expertise to support the dental profession and the people it serves.

Values

1. Members are the purpose of our work. The same is true of communities of interest and coworkers seeking assistance from us in serving our membership. We are all part of the same team, working for the same goals.
   - Membership is everybody's business.
   - Diversity adds value to our community and work.
   - Support the improvement of oral health worldwide.
   - Take pride in dentistry.

2. We take personal responsibility to ensure that all members, potential members, coworkers, and others we serve receive a timely, accurate, and courteous response to their needs.
   - Listen with intent to understand rather than merely intent to reply.
   - Freely share our knowledge.
   - Meet and exceed expectations.
   - Communicate clearly.

3. We take pride in our work.
   - Do the little things and the big things well.
   - Demonstrate zeal for finding solutions.
   - Work diligently, creatively, and effectively.
   - Demonstrate personal dignity, integrity, and dedication.

4. Attitudes are contagious.
   - Extend courtesy and compassion.
   - Be committed and professional.
   - Give praise, recognition, and appreciation often.
   - Lead by example.
   - Have fun: Enjoy our professional life.

5. We thrive in a supportive organization that…
   - Is based upon trust and mutual respect.
   - Facilitates opportunities to learn and grow.
   - Provides the necessary tools and information to do our job.
   - Treats people fairly.
   - Helps us feel that we make a difference and rewards contributions.
   - Applauds innovation and reasonable risk-taking.

entire culture—around assessing and fulfilling members' needs and expectations.

This unity of focus permeates the entire organization. Everyone—staff, leaders, and members alike—knows whom the association serves and keeps the member not only at center stage but also in the spotlight. No one presumes to decide what the member needs without asking first and then listening to the answer.

Because the needs of and the challenges faced by members always take precedence, the way the association replies may seem contrary to its best interest. For example, Associated General Contractors (AGC) changed its dues structure when feedback from chapters indicated the structure was too complicated and the maximum dues cap was too expensive. Lowering dues meant decreasing the association's budget and, consequently, changing how it served members, but AGC took that step in recognition of its members' expressed concerns and as a means of refocusing on its mission.

As another example, the Society for Human Resource Management (SHRM) offers transitional assistance—in the form of a free, one-year membership—to any member laid off from a job. During the U.S. recession of 2008–09, SHRM provided more than 2,000 free memberships annually, even as its own revenues dipped in some areas. For SHRM, helping members survive a layoff trumps a better bottom line. One staff member explained, "We are financially responsible, but we also understand that the core of what we do is the service orientation to our members. They have our full support, even when they are in a difficult situation."

Always on the Lookout

Providing excellent service to members does not translate into "We'll do everything or anything the members ask." It does mean the association makes every effort to understand the members' needs and attempts, within the confines of the mission, to meet them. It means always being on the lookout for the possibilities and opportunities presented by the members' needs and expectations.

In that regard, Girl Scouts of the USA (GSUSA) offers an interesting example. The organization never forgets whom it exists to serve—the girls. In fact, cubicles throughout its headquarters building are decorated with Girl Scouting materials, including photographs of members, as a constant reminder of its vision "to be the premier leadership organization for girls."

Yet, while maintaining absolute clarity about its purpose, GSUSA also understands that its target population is different from its customers—the local councils that facilitate delivery of the Girl Scout program. That's why GSUSA devotes considerable resources to creating software and research monographs, among other resources, that enable the councils to operate effectively.

GSUSA continually asks, "How do we need to change in order to stay true to our mission?" So everything is subject to change, *except for the underlying values.* Consequently, "being the premier leadership organization for girls" means more than organizing traditional troops. The organization has developed flexible pathways for girls to participate, such as delivering the Girl Scout program through suburban after-school programs, urban neighborhood youth centers, and even youth detention centers. Although few people probably associate the Girl Scout mission—"building girls of courage, confidence, and character, who make the world a better place"—with girls incarcerated in detention centers, such a program underscores the organization's ultimate goal to always focus on girl leadership opportunities rather than on a particular image it wants to convey.

This clarity about purpose is marked with a real pragmatism about the means necessary to achieve those ends. GSUSA is every bit as serious and tenacious about putting together the resources, talent, and expertise needed to be effective in addressing its mission as it is passionate about the mission itself. As a case in point, GSUSA's public policy and advocacy agenda explicitly addresses two categories of issues: those that directly affect girls and those that affect the organization's corporate rights.

GOING THE EXTRA MILE FOR MEMBERS

An analysis of membership acquisition and retention numbers shows that the Ohio Society of CPAs (OSCPA) has not suffered wide swings in membership or in participation, even during periods of professional or economic upheaval, when it chooses to give away more services to members. OSCPA even gives away a full year of benefits, in the form of a complimentary membership, to each person who passes the state CPA exam.

To remind members that the association is designed to meet their professional needs, OSCPA goes to extraordinary lengths with its retention efforts. The six-step plan starts with two written notices to members who fail to renew. If necessary, these are followed by up to three personal phone calls, usually from the staff membership vice president, the CEO, and a colleague of the lapsed member. Such a level of personal contact is no small undertaking in a 23,000-member society.

As a last effort, OSCPA sends a surprise message in the form of its monthly magazine. On the outside, the magazine looks identical to the one sent to members in good standing. On the inside, however, the pages are blank except for a message directed exclusively to the lapsed member: "If you had renewed your membership, this magazine would have been full of information and articles that would interest you."

Driven By Mission, Not Money

Measure 2:
Alignment of Products and Services with Mission

The second measure of success is alignment of products and services with mission. Remarkable associations speak passionately about fulfilling their mission and constantly test their ideas for products against that mission, using it as a touchstone for everything they do.

Having a passion for the purpose, however, does not necessarily translate into proficiency. Within the comparison group, we found several instances of organizations whose employees and members exhibited powerful emotion when discussing the association's founding and raison d'être. Even though these organizations had a strong sense of who they originally were, they hadn't effectively harnessed the passion to keep driving forward. In many ways, these associations failed to link the mission to the development of strategic direction, operations, products, and services that would define who they are.

Associations in the study group consistently found ways to connect their reason for being to their programs and services. Most offered, more or less, the usual array of meetings, trade shows, professional publications, educational programs, and affinity programs. Yet while the depth, breadth, and nature of the products and services varied from one remarkable association to another, what didn't change was the consistent focus on linking those offerings to their mission. That focus rarely wavered, even as external forces, societal changes, and developments within the membership itself occurred. In this regard, great associations are truly member-driven.

At GSUSA, for example, the staff and leaders always ask the same central question: What do girls need *today* for us to achieve the mission we have always had? New initiatives and changes to existing programs and services flow from there.

Consider the Radiological Society of North America (RSNA). At one time, RSNA provided association management services to 21 related subgroups or specialties. The society, however, determined that being in the association management business represented a diversion from its mission to educate radiologists and to support radiological research. It took the disciplined but controversial action of releasing all but the three academic societies that were deemed central to its core purpose. The three societies, which focus on advancing radiology in careers, research, and education, now form an academic council within RSNA.

WHAT'S DIFFERENT?

In the intervening five years between editions of this book, four of the nine remarkable associations (44%) experienced a decline in membership. The Ohio Society of CPAs saw declines in several of its membership categories, with a total decrease of about 4 percent. Girl Scouts of the USA experienced a more dramatic decrease, losing about 11 percent of the 3.6 million members it reported in 2006.

Of the other five associations, several registered significant growth. The American College of Cardiology, for example, added 7,000 members—many in new membership categories—and experienced a 54 percent increase in annual revenues. Similarly, the Radiological Society of North America (RSNA) grew by 8,000 members, many of them living outside North America; international members now account for 20 percent of RSNA's membership. Even with this growth, however, RSNA was not recession-proof; its revenues went down in several key categories, notably sales of advertising and exhibit space. To offset these negatives, the society rebid several major contracts to save on costs and changed the terms of some licensing agreements to boost revenue.

RSNA was one of three remarkable associations (33%) that made the commitment not to lay off any staff members during the recession. RSNA, along with Associated General Contractors and the Society for Human Resource Management (SHRM), took the position that layoffs would negatively affect the level of customer service at a time when members most needed the association's assistance; in addition, they wanted to retain their talented workforces so they wouldn't miss a moment of effectively serving members when the economy improved. "Not laying off personnel gave us credibility and loyalty in the eyes of our employees," said a senior executive at SHRM. "We did freeze salaries for one year—but still paid out variable incentive bonuses that year because we met, or exceeded, key performance metrics, such as membership renewals, member satisfaction, and employee engagement."

Six of the associations (66%) have a different CEO from when the Measures of Success study was conducted; at a seventh association, the CEO had announced plans to retire. This brings to mind one of the eligibility criteria used for associations that participated in the study: They were required to have had at least one change in the CEO position within the preceding 15 years. The rationale is that organizational structure and culture contribute more to an association's long-term success than one person's personality, vision, or abilities. In fact, the six remarkable associations that experienced a change in staff leadership since the first edition of *7 Measures of Success* did not miss a beat. At one of those associations, an employee made this telling observation: "Yes, we had a new CEO come in. But if you asked the average member if there had been a change in executive leadership, he or she would say no—because the quality and delivery of products and services haven't changed at all."

An organization in the comparison group found itself in a similar situation of managing special interest groups within the membership. With the association unwilling or unable to decide what to do about these groups, they continued draining its economic reserves, organizational energy, and staff attention. Hence, the association lost the focus on its mission that is needed to achieve greatness.

A Good Fit

Aligning their offerings with their mission enables great associations to do the right things well, even if they fall short on their outcome measures. Make no mistake: Remarkable associations hit their numbers. But they consider themselves successful only if they serve member needs and make progress toward their vision while hitting the numbers.

Remarkable associations view members as a population to serve rather than a market to sell to. In fact, they reject out-of-hand any product or service that fails to directly aid their members, even if it might generate revenue.

The National Association of Counties (NACo) is one organization completely driven by its commitment to meet member needs. If it makes money, so much the better. As one employee noted, "The purpose of a program is the greater good: How can we help counties? Nobody is going to rule out anything that at least meets that criteria."

One of NACo's success stories is the U.S. Communities Government Purchasing Alliance (GPA), which it cosponsors with the Association of School Business Officials International, National Institute of Governmental Purchasing, National League of Cities, and United States Conference of Mayors. GPA grew out of the recognition that counties are chronically short of money. It enables local government agencies to aggregate their purchasing power and obtain volume pricing on office supplies, technology products, janitorial supplies, park equipment, and other categories of supplies. NACo probably could have crafted a group purchasing arrangement on a much smaller scale, such as a typical affinity services program. Doing so, however, would have reduced the organization's effectiveness in meeting its mission.

As co-manager of the program, NACo works with a volunteer advisory group to identify and evaluate the products offered and oversees the competitive bid process to select suppliers. (Vendors with connections to association leaders are excluded from consideration, and elected officials do not intrude on the competitive selection process.)

To market GPA, NACo partners with state associations of counties. NACo estimates that local agencies save approximately 20 percent on their purchases by using the program; in 2011, GPA offered 22 product lines and registered nearly $2 billion in sales.

In addition, NACo offers a supplemental retirement program for county employees, debt-collection services, a human resources consulting service program for employment-related background checks,

---

◆ ◆ ◆ ◆ ◆ ◆ ◆
DEMONSTRATED VALUE

A simple request from a member—"Tell me more about what the association does"—prompted the National Association of Counties (NACo) to begin producing a *Participation and Membership Benefits Report* to accompany its annual dues statement. Customized for each member, the report provides a detailed summary of the services and dollars each county has received as a direct benefit of belonging to NACo.

A county paying $9,000 in annual dues, for example, might learn that it has saved $150,000 in the previous year simply by participating in NACo's Government Purchasing Alliance—in addition to the millions of dollars in federal funds the county may have received because of NACo's lobbying activities. The report also summarizes association involvement, such as how many NACo awards the county has received and the NACo committees on which county employees serve. The computer system built to produce the customized reports enables NACo staff to easily access a county's data and make notes of conversations with and requests by members, so each member interaction can build upon previous interactions to emphasize the association's responsiveness to members and its overall value.

and a service for recovering insurance assets for environmental liabilities. "We try to find niches that aren't being met in the county marketplace," said a NACo employee. "We could make a lot of money selling affinity credit cards, but we don't do that because it doesn't benefit our constituency."

Similarly, a company once approached RSNA with the concept of a permanent, year-round exhibit of radiological equipment that would essentially take the place of RSNA's trade show. RSNA's board gave serious thought to going into business with the company, investing six months and $60,000 to research the proposal. But even after the company offered to double RSNA's payment, the association rejected the proposal. One senior executive described the decision as a simple call: "It clearly was not in our mission," he said.

For NACo, RSNA, and the rest of the study group, the potential for profit is not a prerequisite when considering a product or service. That attitude does not prevail among the comparison associations, where we found several examples of organizations that evaluated products and services primarily based on the potential to generate net revenue.

In one case, an organization with declining dues revenue found itself on the verge of a financial crisis. In its search for options, the association discovered it could obtain federal grants to provide services to organizations in other countries. The influx of cash from these ventures solved the short-term financial crisis but created larger problems with members, who complained, legitimately, that the grant activity was not in line with the organization's mission.

Concentrating its efforts on an activity not related to its mission caused the organization to lose touch with the needs of members and to decrease services to them. Many members, presumably resenting this neglect, chose not to renew their memberships. In the end, the association's efforts did not prevent the financial crisis; they merely delayed it.

◆ ◆ ◆ ◆ ◆ ◆ ◆

A BALANCED PORTFOLIO

Each time an idea for a new product or service surfaces at the Society for Human Resource Management (SHRM), staff ask two questions as part of the association's product development process:

- Has the product or service been thoughtfully considered from a long-term business perspective? In other words, do members really want it? Does it make financial sense?
- How would the potential product or service better serve the member while fitting into the overall portfolio of what SHRM currently offers?

SHRM's director of strategic planning tracks all association products and services, categorizing them by area—such as diversity training or leadership training—and by cost to the member—either for-free (such as the monthly magazine and website access) or for-fee (such as the annual conference and training courses). To receive funding, a proposed idea must survive the scrutiny of the product development process as well as fill an existing gap in SHRM's product portfolio or replace something that has become outdated. No matter how great an idea, it will be temporarily shelved if it will skew the overall benefits portfolio toward a particular area of interest or cost to members.

In another case, an association in the comparison group had a history of initiating programs that appeared to be good ideas from a financial standpoint but inevitably didn't hit the mark with either members' needs or the marketplace. Some, for example, were seen by state associations as directly competing for the same target market and thus became sources of tension. The programs' lack of success may have resulted from a deficient understanding of members and the marketplace.

During interviews, staff at this association acknowledged that, in their search for products and services, they always placed a priority on what would make money—and the more money, the better. Members' needs are almost an afterthought. Despite this financial orientation, the association still finds itself in a penny-pinching mode most years.

"There's a real sense here that the focus is just on high-revenue things," said one employee. "A lot of times [members] have ideas that are financially not feasible, but when we hear from them we try to make what we're doing meet their needs."

No Fear of Failure

To find the right mix of products and services that align with their missions, remarkable associations willingly engage in experimentation. They doggedly protect their core purpose and related activities while investigating new initiatives. What's more, they fully expect many of their efforts to fall flat. As one employee at NACo noted, "We think of programs as pancakes. You ought to be able to throw the first two away."

Far from being facetious, this employee was simply reflecting the cultural norms at NACo, where failures of products and services are not swept under the carpet. Instead, staff and volunteers openly analyze failures to extract lessons learned and identify possible ways to repurpose the information or the concept.

The willingness to experiment—and fail—in their quest to better serve members is evident throughout the study group. For the most part, interviewees from these remarkable associations spoke openly and candidly about the products and services that fell far short of expectations for whatever reason: failure to attract attendees, to resonate with the majority of members, or to generate enough revenue for sustaining the venture. They also talked about the systems they have in place to evaluate and improve their offerings.

Much of the experimentation involves harnessing the power of technology to provide additional touchpoints with members. For example, acknowledging its members' growing use of electronic media, the American Dental Association (ADA) released several of its best-selling print titles as e-books and designed an application for smartphones and tablets that allows for quick and easy checking of insurance billing codes. Another mobile application, offered free to ADA members who attend the association's annual meeting, enables them to conduct searches for exhibits and product listings, set up appointments, and access information on show specials. It also includes links to association events, continuing education speakers, Facebook, and Twitter.

Research conducted by AARP revealed that social networking was becoming a bigger part of everyday life for its members as well. The results prompted one senior executive to observe, "AARP must deliver the same reliable information and first-rate resources we always have, but in a more interactive way, when and where AARP.org users and online community members want it." In response, AARP overhauled its website to enable users to share content seamlessly between the online community and other social networking sites. In addition, AARP decided to make much of its online content available on e-readers, smartphones, and other handheld devices.

Since 2006—the same year Twitter made its debut and YouTube celebrated its first birthday—the Ohio Society of CPAs (OSCPA) has increasingly pushed information, photos, and video to social media sites, which the organization thinks will play a huge role for driving interest and participation in its educational offerings. During the 2008 recession, even as its advertising revenue declined and members paid their dues more slowly than in previous years, OSCPA did not pull back from the investment in social media. Of these efforts an OSCPA senior executive says, "Are we getting high levels of participation and engagement from members? No—but we are working diligently to encourage that."

Another remarkable association started delivering content through a variety of mobile applications, relying on a staff task force to identify potential business models for each application. Notes the CEO, "We don't wait until something is perfect to get it out there."

GO OR NO-GO

"This organization gives us permission to try something new and not succeed. They embrace good ideas and work on them."

— National Association of Counties

"So few things have been launched that it would be hard to have any flops."

— Matched-pair comparison association

Adaptability, as described in greater detail later in this book, is a hallmark of remarkable associations. But with experimentation comes a built-in commitment to analysis, to continuous learning. Remarkable associations do not believe in permanent pilot programs; they do not spend years trying to make a failed effort work. At AARP, an employee in the research department explained, "We have had our share of products that have not been successful from the start, but we change them based on our research and findings. We learn from mistakes. We either pull the product or restructure the product and launch it again."

RSNA also acknowledges that missteps occur, even though it follows an assessment process before giving the go-ahead to a new project or product. When asked how the association deals with product failures, one RSNA employee simply observed, "People talk about it and laugh and learn from it."

Employees at associations in the comparison group were rarely that forthcoming in interviews conducted by the research investigators. In addition to being reluctant to discuss product and program failures, they usually could not describe what the association learned or did differently as a result.

CHAPTER 3

Commitment to Analysis and Feedback

*Commitment to Analysis and Feedback:
Consistently exhibiting data-driven strategies
and dialogue and engagement, with a CEO who
serves as a broker of ideas.*

REMARKABLE ASSOCIATIONS make a practice of aligning their products and services with their mission and keeping members at the center of their universe. But how do they know whether they have hit the mark or missed by a mile? By asking over and over, again and again, in every conceivable way.

Associations in the study group were continually learning about the environment in which they and their members operate. They didn't restrict themselves to formal research—which all did and did well—but looked for every opportunity to hold conversations with members and encourage dialogue between staff and volunteers. Then they actually did something with the information they had gathered, such as modifying a product, introducing a new service, or initiating change through board dialogue and deliberation. We also found that the CEO, in one way or another, took an active interest in making sure something happened.

THE 7 MEASURES OF SUCCESS

Commitment to Purpose
1. A Customer Service Culture
2. Alignment of Products and Services with Mission

Commitment to Analysis and Feedback
3. Data-Driven Strategies
4. Dialogue and Engagement
5. CEO as a Broker of Ideas

Commitment to Action
6. Organizational Adaptability
7. Alliance Building

Data, Data, Data

Measure 3: Data-Driven Strategies

If there's one phrase that sets remarkable associations apart from their counterparts, it's "data, data, data." They gather information, analyze it, and then use it to become even better. Research—whether quantitative or qualitative, formal or anecdotal—is always put to use, not put on the shelf.

The third measure, data-driven strategies, refers to a continuous loop that remarkable associations tend to exhibit: They continually track member needs and issues as well as the wider environment, then collectively analyze the data to reach a shared understanding through asking, "What do we now know? What are we going to do about it?" These associations then incorporate the findings into their strategic and operational planning.

But the data collection doesn't stop there. It continues through another methodical, disciplined cycle of gathering, analyzing, and making changes because of what was learned.

Girl Scouts of the USA (GSUSA), for instance, constantly researches the societal trends that affect and influence its reason for being: the girls. Some fact finding is done through the Girl Scout Research Institute, a separate entity that focuses on informed public policy making. GSUSA's market research function handles other projects, including data calibration with the U.S. Census office.

"How are the needs and experiences of girls changing?" Every time GSUSA asks that question, it makes a commitment to seeing the world with new eyes. The organization communicates research results vertically and horizontally, at the national and local levels, and to staff as well as volunteers. This process leads to the development of contemporary programs that appeal to today's girls.

Over the years, GSUSA's data-driven strategies have led to a variety of initiatives, including numerous programs aimed at helping girls develop math and financial literacy skills, a mentoring partnership to link girls with female scientists, and an antiviolence education initiative. Also, by keeping a close watch on census data, GSUSA was able to respond early on—with targeted, bilingual materials and special programs—to an increase in Hispanic girls in America.

In contrast, a comparison association did not do the research that would have opened its leaders' eyes to coming population changes and their potential effect on the organization's traditional membership base. Because it was slow to develop programs aimed at anyone other than its traditional members, the organization has struggled with membership attrition as well as brand identity. It lost momentum by not researching environmental and membership trends and examining how to adapt while remaining true to its mission.

"Having data to guide you, so you know when issues are coming up, is powerful. It ensures your organization is not only prepared ahead of time but also able to help members understand the context for the painful and hard decisions that may need to be made," believes an employee of SHRM.

The value of being data-driven was confirmed for SHRM when the 2008 recession arrived. The association had identified early warning indicators among the many metrics it tracks and had prepared several contingency plans to implement, dependent on the severity of the recession and how it affected SHRM's top-line and bottom-line revenues as well as operating income. "Because we are so data-driven, we weren't flying by the seat of our pants," the employee continues. "We had a very good idea of what direction we were headed financially and knew what we needed to cut back on if the situation worsened." SHRM shared its various contingency plans widely so neither staff nor members would be surprised if the organization revised or even discontinued certain services, programs, or benefits.

DUE DILIGENCE

Some simple internal research and analysis might have prevented one association in the comparison group from making financial missteps that had long-lasting repercussions.

In one instance, it decided to partner with a website developer that did not have the financial stability to implement an e-commerce initiative as promised. The association not only lost money but also lost momentum toward improving its online presence for several years.

In another instance, the association spun off its most lucrative division into a separate entity but did not retain an ongoing financial interest in the new entity. One employee described this decision as "giving away the cash cow" and, indeed, the association struggled for years to overcome the subsequent loss of revenue.

Beyond the formal market research or environmental scanning done by associations in the study group, we found a commitment to mining data from just about every encounter with members.

The staff and leaders at remarkable associations are constantly listening to members and sharing the information they glean from those contacts. Remarkable associations also face the facts: They're not so arrogant as to presume that they know better than what the data tell them. When new data demonstrate that the present course, no matter how well conceived, is in error, remarkable associations do not hesitate to make adjustments. An employee of the American College of Cardiology (ACC) put it this way: "We do market research, we do feasibility studies, because that way we can bring data to the board. We don't just run with something because it sounds like a great idea."

♦ ♦ ♦ ♦ ♦ ♦ ♦

HOMEWORK VERSUS GUESSWORK

"We ask a lot of questions, through interactions with our members and staff and through research and surveys. That's how we learn more about our members."

— Society for Human Resource Management

"No, we don't do any formal scanning or research."
— Matched-pair comparison association

Integrated Systems

Here are additional data-driven examples culled from the study group:

• ACC has two groups that do environmental scanning. Each member of the internal (staff) group focuses on tracking trends in one of five major areas, such as demographics or economics, that ACC has deemed essential to its future. Members forming an external group periodically review the trend information to add insights from their perspectives. ACC's chapters also provide trend observations. All the results contribute to the development of annual initiatives and long-term strategic goals.

The executive committee, which also serves as the strategic planning committee, assigns several metrics, or key measures, to each of ACC's strategic goals. These key measures include statistical performance of publications and conferences (attendance, readership scores, abstract submissions), membership numbers (satisfaction scores, retention), customer service metrics (call center waiting times, website access), and financial performance (revenue growth, revenue diversification). Each quarter, ACC's leaders evaluate the annual initiatives in view of the progress made on strategic goals and make adjustments as needed.

◆ ◆ ◆ ◆ ◆ ◆ ◆

DIGGING DEEPER INTO THE NUMBERS

Despite being recognized as a remarkable association, the Ohio Society of CPAs (OSCPA) did not rest on its laurels. Shortly after the initial publication of *7 Measures of Success* in 2006, the society launched an organization-wide self-assessment. Each employee received a copy of the book to read in preparation for departmental and full-staff discussions on how well OSCPA performed on each of the seven measures. The weakest performance, staff agreed, came in the area of data-driven strategies.

That realization led to the implementation of a new database system that enables individual staff members to access and subdivide the data they need to customize communications or target marketing messages. In addition, the society created a new position dedicated to data analysis. "Becoming more aggressively data-driven in our activities has helped us decide what products or services to play up—and to whom—what to play down, and what to develop more fully," said a senior executive. For example, when analyses of attendance at continuing education programs revealed that members actually had a much broader spectrum of interests than they reported on membership surveys, OSCPA refined its marketing efforts—and program registrations grew. OSCPA also retooled its entire website—and continually tweaks the design—based on in-depth analyses of the information and areas that members access the most.

• In addition to ongoing focus groups and surveys, including consumer opinion polls, the American Dental Association (ADA) relies on its 11 councils to study and report on issues relating to a specific area of interest. Recommendations are forwarded to the board of trustees. Given its history of refining internal and volunteer structures to better align to strategic needs and opportunities, ADA seems to adapt its structure to fit needs rather than try to fit issues into its existing structure.

- The Society for Human Resource Management (SHRM) routinely conducts readership and advertising surveys, member needs assessments, member perception surveys, research about the workplace environment, and analyses of website usage, as well as product evaluations and informal discussions with members.

  SHRM also maintains a sophisticated database that enables it to track member activity. "We look at what books they are buying, what they are doing, what questions they are asking, what resources they use," said one staff member. "We analyze as much information as possible as a way of serving them better and understanding their needs."

  SHRM put the detailed data to good use in 2010 when it revisited its "membership bundle"—all the goods and services provided free to dues-paying members. After an in-depth review of what members were actually using, SHRM retired several offerings, including an annual trends symposium, white papers, and online glossaries. The membership bundle was then modified to include new products and services that addressed areas in which members had demonstrated greater interest.

- Associated General Contractors (AGC) posts surveys on its website that ask members a variety of questions about potential products and services: Are you interested in this product? How much would you pay for this service? What format would you prefer? Is this important for your business? The results are analyzed to determine the costs and time involved, whether an author or someone else is needed to develop the product, and a production timeline.

"We know who the product is for, who the market is, before production even begins," said one employee. "And the businesses that buy our products know we have done our research."

Added another AGC employee, "Through surveys and studies, we ensure we're making decisions based on solid data, rather than on someone's opinion or whim."

◆ ◆ ◆ ◆ ◆ ◆ ◆
PUT TO THE TEST

AARP might well represent the gold standard for association research. Everything it does is driven by research, research, and more research. Much of the data gathering is designed and implemented by AARP's internal research department, which focuses on three main areas: Medicare and health, marketing and membership, and environmental scanning of all types.

AARP conducts annual employee satisfaction surveys, employee exit interviews, member focus groups, telephone surveys, opinion polls, product evaluation surveys, and studies of ethnographics and econometrics. It tracks media coverage and the performance of its partnerships and affiliations. Through an outside call center, it keeps tabs on membership needs and interests, brand recognition, approval and product satisfaction ratings, and advocacy issues. AARP knows its members so well that it can tell you how often they take vacations, what airline they fly most frequently, and where they prefer to shop.

No product or service is released to the market without first undergoing an extensive, structured research process. As one employee explained, "We have learned not to act unless we are sure of the outcomes." The process typically includes a pilot test of both the product and its marketing, followed by an evaluative focus group. If something isn't quite right, AARP repackages or repositions the product and does additional market testing.

Relying on research-based information to guide strategic and tactical decisions at all levels has affected AARP both externally and internally. Noted one employee, "External changes include better member satisfaction and making the right decisions. For internal purposes, we look at ways to streamline processes and operating efficiencies. Employees and members are better satisfied, and the organization is better aligned with [its] strategic goals and objectives."

Given the research expertise it has developed, it's not surprising that AARP also participates in a joint venture, a for-profit research company, that focuses on the population aged 50 and over.

The online surveys supplement formal research into member satisfaction and needs, environmental and competitive trends, and economic forecasting done by AGC's staff economist. All are part of AGC's disciplined approach to new initiatives, which includes earmarking a percentage of its annual marketing budget for business/product development. AGC also sets specific goals in this area (for example, "increase product-line revenue by an average of 10 percent each year"). Over a 10-year period that began in the 1990s, such steps helped AGC reduce its dependence on membership dues as a part of total income by 26 percent.

We also noticed that employees at remarkable associations usually can clearly articulate who their competition is and often recite precise percentages of any membership overlap between their organization and the competition.

MINING DATA FOR MEMBERS' USE

The American College of Cardiology (ACC) has a long history of translating science into data-based tools for use by its members, including appropriate use criteria; performance measures; and guidelines that set standards of care for diagnosing, managing, and preventing cardiovascular disease. The association also took the lead in building and maintaining registries of patient outcomes. Each year, it spends millions of dollars to collect the data that help determine which type of care translates into the best clinical outcomes for patients. These registries, which hospitals pay a fee to access, enable cardiologists and other cardiovascular healthcare professionals to provide the highest quality care possible.

Similarly, Girl Scouts of the USA (GSUSA) drew on its extensive research findings to craft a leadership experience for girls based on 15 outcomes—specific skills and values that every girl who participates in Girl Scouting can expect to gain. Examples of these outcomes include developing critical thinking skills, becoming a resourceful problem solver, and feeling empowered to make a difference in the world. Then, to determine how well the organization is achieving these outcomes, GSUSA developed an online assessment tool for use by volunteer leaders. Various indicators, based on age level, will help the Girl Scout leaders measure girls' progress on the outcomes and overall leadership development.

The Ohio Society of CPAs (OSCPA) even has a group of members who volunteer to attend the courses offered by competitors and report on their experiences. "They tell us what they saw, the differences between our programs and others', and how we can be better or more effective," said one staff member.

In short, remarkable associations continuously and vigorously do their homework.

Ongoing Conversations

Measure 4: Dialogue and Engagement

Although remarkable associations have developed an expertise in gathering information, they know that's not enough. They also nurture a culture in which the information is analyzed and shared throughout the organization. Everyone, not just senior managers and elected leaders, is expected to use that data to figure out what actions the data are demanding of the organization.

The fourth measure, dialogue and engagement, is characterized by a close-knit, consistent culture where all employees not only receive the same script, in the form of the same information, but also see the potential to contribute to a blockbuster production. Whether they have lead or supporting roles or work behind the scenes is not relevant. Rather, they all share equally in the responsibility to contribute and add value to the association.

This culture is the natural outgrowth of what numerous interviewees described as "constant communication." Many within the study group would no doubt echo the employee at the Society for Human Resource Management (SHRM) who said, "We all discuss decisions openly with each other. We have a desire to collaborate with each other, and we do it in mission-driven ways.

"We aren't competitive here with each other," continued the same employee. "We are here to serve the same people and do what's best for the profession." That desire to always put the organization first, before individual or departmental gain, was displayed repeatedly in the study group.

STRUCTURED TO SHARE

In 1999, the Radiological Society of North America (RSNA) moved into new headquarters that proved to be an extension of its team-oriented approach. Designed by staff, the award-winning space has all the traditional components of an association headquarters—separate offices, cubicles, meeting rooms, and so forth—but it has a brighter, more open, and more energetic feel than most.

RSNA's offices occupy two floors, which are joined by an open staircase. All outside walls feature floor-to-ceiling windows and all offices have glass walls and doors, enabling natural light to reach every workspace. (The only offices with opaque doors belong to the magazine staff, who requested a minimum of visual distractions.)

Outside the large central reception area are four identical offices for RSNA's four assistant executive directors. The offices' central location gives all employees the opportunity to easily see and visit with these senior staff members. The CEO's office is nearby, also easily accessible to all staff.

Demolishing the Silos

Remarkable associations generally do not exhibit what's typically referred to as the silo mentality—organizational fragmentation by department or responsibility. When asked about signature products, for example, employees of great associations usually gave the same answers no matter what department they worked in or what their supervisory level. They shared a common view of who the association was and how well it served its members.

Contrast that clear understanding of organization identity and purpose with the confusion often displayed among employees of associations in the comparison group. Within that group, staff in different departments typically identified different signature products—usually the ones in their own area. At one association, for instance, a senior staff director said, "[The association]'s signature products and services and the ones in my area are very different." Another employee at the same association responded, "The signature products and services are different depending on whether you classify them by revenue or by the customer."

Remarkable associations avoid this type of segregation. For them, everything is about the members. Therefore, they ensure internal dialogue continually takes place throughout the organization about its

---

EVERYONE AT THE TABLE

By all accounts, the board and staff of the American College of Cardiology (ACC) have always had a solid, respectful relationship. "What has changed is what the staff can contribute—and that's no longer just the logistics of organizational arrangements," reported one long-time employee. "Now there's more of a partnership between staff and the board in terms of feedback about the marketplace. Staff focus on how we can give the board the data they need to set direction. The board still makes the decisions but asks more for [our] opinions and input."

The change was made consciously by a CEO and an elected president who wanted to increase board effectiveness. In addition to clarifying board and staff roles, they revamped the physical layout used for board meetings. Previously, the 30-member board sat in alphabetical order; the elected president sat at the head of the table, marked by the presence of a lectern. Participation was somewhat perfunctory, with most board members simply reading reports. The arrangement relegated senior staff to the perimeter of the room; if called on to speak, they had to walk up to the lectern.

ACC stopped assigning seats, freeing the elected president, CEO, and staff vice presidents to sit among the board members. The tenor of the board meetings changed along with the physical arrangements: Board members became more engaged with one another and with staff. Typically, after reviewing progress on ACC's strategic plan and its financial status, the board members and senior staff break into small groups to discuss policy positions or other strategic issues.

"The meetings are much more interesting, with people asking more questions," one employee reported. "The board is thinking broader about strategy and decisions for the whole organization."

---

direction, priorities, and reason for being (serving members). Here are some examples of how they do that:

- Within five weeks of their starting date, new employees of OSCPA meet with the CEO, who explains the organization's vision and goals. Periodically, the entire staff assembles for a review of OSCPA's annual goals and a progress report.

- The National Association of Counties (NACo) regularly holds "County 101" sessions with its national staff (and vendor members, too, if requested) to help ensure that everyone is clear about what its members do.

  To emphasize the importance of information sharing throughout the organization, NACo holds weekly meetings in which staff are expected to talk to one another about how their various areas intersect and interact. It also holds cross-functional team retreats to ensure activities not only align with the strategic plan but also complement one another.

  "We've gotten rid of the silo mentality internally," explained one director. "Every department used to operate so autonomously that there wasn't a working relationship between any of them. Now, we coordinate efforts."

- As at many associations, the Society for Human Resource Management's (SHRM's) employees gather once a month to welcome new hires and celebrate employment anniversaries, but they also hear an update about the state of the association. During this all-staff meeting, the CEO reviews overall goals and discusses what SHRM is doing as an organization to meet those goals.

- At the Radiological Society of North America (RSNA), informal meetings between the CEO and small groups of employees (10 to 12 staff members of varying tenure) revealed that, due to rapid membership growth, newer employees did not fully understand the organization's mission nor communicate well across departments. To remedy the situation, RSNA launched an intranet accessible by all staff. Updated weekly, the intranet summarizes activities throughout the society and serves as a conduit for widespread sharing of information. In addition, RSNA periodically hosts brown-bag sessions where employees gather for lunch and an informal discussion of various departments' responsibilities and activities.

Thanks to such ongoing dialogues, staff members at remarkable associations not only understand their own roles but also understand and appreciate the roles of their colleagues. All employees share a strong commitment to the notion that "We are here for the members." Departmental boundaries and petty turf wars give way to a shared drive to deliver high quality products and services that address member needs and deliver on the mission.

Moreover, remarkable associations effectively maintain a class-less structure. Rather than focusing on distinctions between executive and staff or profit centers and service areas, these organizations reflect a neighborhood culture characterized by shared values and a unified purpose.

Remarkable associations often extend dialogue and engagement to their relationships with members. As an example, the Ohio Society of CPAs (OSCPA) literally takes to the road to hear what its members think. In addition to conducting a "listening tour"—visiting the 100 largest employers of its members in the state—the association sponsors professional issues updates in both the spring and the fall. Typically presented by the CEO, each 3½-hour session provides the society's perspective or interpretation of a pressing issue or two and features an extended and unstructured question-and-answer period with members. The programs, which attract as many as 500 attendees per location, rank among the top membership benefits on OSCPA's member satisfaction surveys.

A MODEL OF COLLABORATION

At Associated General Contractors (AGC), management doesn't just talk about the importance of working as a team. They also model the behavior through a unique "shared responsibility" arrangement between the CEO and COO.

Both positions report directly to the board, are similarly compensated, and have equal standing in the eyes of members and staff. The difference is that the CEO focuses primarily on external affairs while the COO concentrates on internal operations. The two leaders, whom the board hired as a team following the short tenure of the previous CEO, describe their roles as "business partners." Employees are not confused by the unusual leadership structure but see it as a model for collaborative decision making throughout the organization.

The Great Go-Between

Measure 5: CEO as a Broker of Ideas

No matter how good the script, an interactive dialogue among all the players is unlikely to occur without a director—in this case, the association's chief executive officer. The association leader must not only understand the organization's vision but also be able to engage others in defining, refining, and responding to that vision and all it entails.

While CEOs may certainly be visionary leaders, what's more important is their ability to facilitate visionary thinking throughout the organization. What sets the study group apart from the comparison group is the fifth measure of success: the CEO as a broker of ideas.

To CEOs of remarkable associations, what matters is not their vision for the association but rather the members' vision. To be sure, the CEO plays a key role in creating a vision for the organization. That role, however, rests with gathering consensus around a member-generated vision rather than forcing buy-in into a personal vision.

All the associations that participated in the study, no matter which research group they were in, had transitioned away from an autocratic, controlling CEO at some point in the preceding 20 years. Stories were told of former CEOs who edited every communication sent by the association, pitted department directors against one another in mean-spirited competition, played favorites among staff and members, and even hand-picked which flowers to plant at the association's headquarters. Those days are gone—although not necessarily long gone.

Virtually all the CEOs whose associations participated in the Measures of Success project were described as fostering a "team" or "family" environment within the association and as being willing to listen to others' ideas. Yet having the ability to listen and be open to others' ideas isn't enough. The CEO must also stimulate energy and engagement among and between staff and volunteers and be willing to step aside at times to facilitate a discussion of ideas without dictating an outcome.

In remarkable associations, the CEO helps both elected leaders and staff think in terms of what is possible and enables things to happen rather than decreeing what will happen. Staff input is both welcomed and respected, with no apparent class distinctions giving more weight to some employees' ideas over others'.

An example from the comparison group helps put this measure in context. One association made a concerted effort to dismantle a longstanding bureaucracy in which ideas had to work their way up through the chain of command. Many ideas died along the way, which had dampened further creativity. Despite the introduction of cross-functional teams, staff continued to believe that senior managers would block innovations, so they took new ideas directly to the CEO.

Rather than open an organizational dialogue, the CEO primarily communicated with the employee or member who had brought forward the idea, bypassing input from other staff and members. As a result, the CEO actually undermined any efforts to foster innovation and teamwork. Distrust among staff and departments was the norm—to the point where employees were reluctant to attend meetings on other departments' "turf"—so sharing ideas did not occur easily. Perhaps not surprisingly, the association introduced few new products and services.

In this association, as in several other comparison associations, the CEO seemed isolated and had a different view of the organizational culture than most of the employees who were interviewed. In contrast, CEOs in the study group generally avoided being isolated by themselves, with senior staff, or with a group of elected officers. They took pains to clarify the roles and responsibilities expected of everyone—board, staff, and CEO—in the association partnership.

CHAPTER 4

Commitment to Action

Commitment to Action:
Consistently exhibiting organizational
adaptability and alliance building.

Textbook strategic plans—complete with clearly outlined goals, objectives, and strategies that were reviewed and adjusted on a consistent basis—were present in many of the associations that participated in the Measures of Success study. Interestingly, these textbook plans were most common in the *comparison* group.

That's not to say that the associations in the study group are not strategic in determining who they are or where they are headed. On the contrary, as underscored in Chapters 2 and 3, remarkable associations never look away from their members. They amass data, engage in ongoing dialogues, and design products and services to support and serve those members. Make no mistake: These associations are truly strategic. All of them depend on a strategic plan, although theirs are often less formal than the plans of the comparison associations.

The difference is that remarkable associations don't simply emphasize thinking strategically. They find it equally important to *act* strategically; they consistently implement their priorities.

Associations in the study group may not have had as well-crafted or well-documented plans, but everyone—volunteers and staff alike—understood what the plan and goals were and lived them.

The comprehensive strategic plans of associations in the comparison group, in contrast, often ran contrary to their eventual actions or inactions. Within the comparison group, the associations often failed to act in ways that would advance their strategic priorities. That is, their magnificently crafted, comprehensive strategic plans resulted in little real change in the organization or the extent to which it served its members. Similarly, several comparison associations frequently revised their strategic plans, yet little about the organization actually changed.

In other words, among remarkable associations, it matters what you do, not just what you say.

"We are not a sitting-still organization but an action organization." This statement, spoken by an employee of the Society for Human Resource Management (SHRM), reflects the mindset of all nine study organizations.

◆ ◆ ◆ ◆ ◆ ◆ ◆

THE 7 MEASURES OF SUCCESS

Commitment to Purpose
1. A Customer Service Culture
2. Alignment of Products and Services with Mission

Commitment to Analysis and Feedback
3. Data-Driven Strategies
4. Dialogue and Engagement
5. CEO as a Broker of Ideas

Commitment to Action
6. Organizational Adaptability
7. Alliance Building

The Will to Act

Measure 6: Organizational Adaptability

Among the participating associations, a high percentage experienced at least one crisis during the 15-year study period, typically a financial setback or a leadership void. The comparison organizations tended to react more slowly than the study organizations. It seemed to take them longer not only to understand what was happening but also to determine the best course of action. A frequent response was to continue what they were already doing; they simply worked harder or more intensely, hoping the extra effort would resolve the crisis.

Remarkable associations demonstrated the sixth measure, organizational adaptability, by not only weathering crises but also learning from them. In the face of markedly declining membership or program revenue, for example, study organizations quickly assessed the situation and then took action—with no excuses.

The economic slowdown of the early 1990s certainly affected Associated General Contractors (AGC), which registered its highest rate of membership attrition in 1992. AGC realized that it could no longer afford to maintain its staffing levels or its headquarters building and lost no time in making the tough, but necessary, calls. In addition to making staff cutbacks, it sold the building—not a highly popular decision—and relocated to rented quarters for more than a decade.

During the 2008-09 recession, which hit the construction industry particularly hard, AGC's members reported a 20 percent unemployment rate. Facing the possibility of membership attrition, AGC again responded quickly. The association cut its budget by 10 percent, instituted a salary freeze for two years, and expanded online learning opportunities to reduce members' need to travel. AGC made a conscious decision not to lay off staff so the organization could continue offering the same, pre-recession level of service to members.

Membership decreased, primarily in the service provider/supplier category, but AGC retained 90 percent of its contractor members, who clearly see value in their membership even when economic times are tough.

Years earlier, the National Association of Counties (NACo) had found itself in a deficit situation. In one year, it cut a $2.5 million deficit by $900,000 by taking decisive action. NACo instituted a hiring freeze, slashed staff travel, and cut other expenditures across the board. "We started right away, which is why we were able to pay off the debt," recalled one employee. The association also expanded its for-profit operations, an action that paid big dividends more than a decade later. NACo's for-profit operations have grown to account for 48 percent of its revenues; its wider array of revenue sources helped the association weather the 2008–09 recession without needing to make significant budget cuts or raise dues.

When faced with financial challenges, both AGC and NACo moved quickly to adapt to a new reality. Both associations also approached a financial crisis as a learning experience so they could avoid such situations in the future. Even when the 2008 recession arrived, both organizations remained disciplined in their budgeting and planning processes and did not waver from financial goals they had established years earlier.

That discipline paid off. For example, in the 1990s, AGC established the long-term goal of having at least 50 percent of its income come from nondues sources; by 2011, nondues revenue represented 47 percent of annual income, and the association remained committed to meeting its goal. After recovering its financial footing in the early 1990s, NACo decided to build a reserve equal to slightly more than one year's operating budget—a goal it achieved in 2006 and continues to maintain. In fact, the association's reserves almost tripled in size from 1999 to 2009, even as the faltering economy had begun battering its member counties.

NACo also revamped its budgeting process to increase board ownership of the organization's fiscal health. Although NACo staff prepare the budget, members of the executive, finance, and auditing committees review it during a special meeting. "They get a very detailed picture of what we're spending money on, and they can ask any questions they'd like," explained one employee. "We also talk about salaries [in the aggregate] and discuss any trends. We involve them as much as possible, so the board isn't just getting a budget handed to them by staff."

Prune to Grow

Overall, the study group exhibited an unwavering determination to terminate programs that do not contribute to the mission. The study associations subject all of their programs and activities to intense scrutiny. Nothing is considered an entitlement or a sacred cow whose worth goes unquestioned.

Some examples from the study associations illustrate this point:

- In the late 1990s, the Ohio Society of CPAs (OSCPA) made a significant organizational change. The society's board voted to eliminate its chapters, thus creating one state level of dues.

  This decision, recommended by two grassroots task forces, was based on the belief that the chapter structure did not contribute member value and detracted from OSCPA's ability to provide core services. Dissolving the chapters gave OSCPA direct access to all of its members and provided more direct communication and delivery of services. Although controversial, this decision came to be accepted as the right thing to do among the majority of OSCPA members.

- Although the American College of Cardiology (ACC) encouraged its members to embrace change and work together to shape the future of healthcare, a long-time policy dissuaded its staff from doing the same. Specifically, most employees enjoyed the privilege of telecommuting four days per week. Their empty desks baffled visiting members; after all, cardiologists don't work alone or from home. When the association curtailed the telecommuting policy to one day per week, a good number of long-time employees resented the change and resigned. The ones who remained, however, became more open to bouncing ideas off of one another—and more likely to be available when a member drops by for a visit.

• SHRM engages in what the author Peter Drucker referred to as "purposeful abandonment." Each year, teams of staff members present their evaluations of existing and proposed products and services. Programs or services that are judged to no longer meet the needs of members are either revised or dropped and replaced with something new. "A lot of what we do is growth through selected mutation. Sometimes products are reinvented to adapt to new changes," explained one employee.

SHRM also changed its board selection process as part of its focus on continuous improvement. As the organization continued to grow and change, SHRM needed specific skills and competencies on its board to ensure the growth continued.

Previously, SHRM volunteers had worked in volunteer capacities that were progressively larger or more national in scope before becoming board members. The process SHRM put in place requires members to apply for a seat on the board of directors; they submit resumés and go through interviews—a process much like the one members themselves use on the job. "Board members are chosen based on their skills and qualifications and how well they meet certain criteria," explained one staff member.

• Every time they attend a management retreat, NACo's senior staff members devote a half-day to talking about which programs they should introduce, what they should modify or adapt in some way, and what they should stop doing completely. Staff then look to members to validate their recommendations, by comparing the three lists to data gathered through membership surveys and other research vehicles.

REVISITING THE PAST—OR LIVING IN IT

"Programs are very easy to add, but they're hard to get out of. So three years down the road, if we're still doing it, people ask, 'Why?'"

– National Association of Counties

"Generally, we do the same products and services we've done for a long time.... This organization protects the status quo. It doesn't like to change much."

– Matched-pair comparison association

Mission Sensitive

As willing as they are to change, remarkable associations know what *not* to change. Their mission and purpose remain the touchstones. They understand that what is needed to serve their core purpose changes as the environment in which they operate changes.

Girl Scouts of the USA (GSUSA) has never veered away from its mission to serve girls. But GSUSA *has* changed the wording of its bedrock Promise and Law, the ways in which it communicates with girls, the methods used to deliver the Girl Scout program (not just traditional troops), and its uniforms (numerous redesigns to stay contemporary), to name a few examples.

The Brownie uniform worn in 2011 certainly looks different from the one worn in 1961 or even 1991, but what that uniform represents hasn't changed. GSUSA, like most of the study associations, constantly engages in the balancing act of remaining true to its mission while investigating and implementing adaptations to its operations

REALIGNMENT TO REMAIN RELEVANT

"What can I do to help Girl Scouting remain the premier leadership experience for girls?"

That's the question GSUSA put to all its constituents in order to develop its Core Business Strategy—an in-depth look at how Girl Scouting needed to transform itself to remain relevant and successful in the future.

To encourage dialogue among its members, GSUSA set up a special website and email link related to the Core Business Strategy and invited them to "be willing to do things differently and strive to makes the changes that will result in the future we seek." At the same time, members were reassured, "[The Girl Scout Promise and Law] are tied to the rich history of Girl Scouts, and they will continue to be at the heart of the Girl Scout experience." At one of its triennial conventions, GSUSA hosted an "open space conversation" so national delegates could discuss this question: "What would our governance structure look like on a national and local level if it met the test of being efficient, decisive, and action-oriented?"

Members' feedback was provided to a 26-member strategy team. The team embarked on a detailed situation analysis, which included answering these four questions:

1. What is the environment in which we must compete and win?
2. What do we want to achieve, and how will we measure success?
3. What are those few things we must do outstandingly well in order to win in this environment?
4. How will we align the organization and inspire our people to achieve superior execution?

After looking at the market it served, its competitors, socioeconomic trends, and alternative revenue models, GSUSA confronted what its chief executive called "a number of brutal truths." Those challenges included a heavy dependence on internal funding; a bureaucratic, slow-moving decision-making process; and a tradition-bound, internally focused culture.

Next, GSUSA appointed six "gap" teams to find ways to close the gap between the organization's current status (as defined by the brutal truths) and where it wanted to be (defined as strategic priorities). The strategic teams, each having

Continues on next page

and services. The organization values its history and tradition but acknowledges that what worked yesterday is not always relevant to what will work today.

Continued from previous page

members from all organizational levels, functions, and geographic regions, focused on Program, Volunteerism, Brand, Funding, Governance Structure, and Organizational Culture. One outcome of the teams' work was the realization that GSUSA's local councils needed to be better structured to reflect 21st century realities; many councils, for example, diverged widely in size, funding, effectiveness, and number of girls served. As an example, the largest 20 percent of councils served 50 percent of the total number of girls in Girl Scouting; the smallest 20 percent of councils served 5 percent of girls.

In 2006, with the assistance of demography experts, the organization radically redrew the jurisdictions of its local councils so each would meet similar criteria (such as population served, size of media market, and median household income). Over a three-year period, GSUSA merged its 312 local councils into 112—a 64 percent reduction. The national organization did not impose the realignment but rather collaborated with its local councils by providing detailed data on demographics and the competitive environment, along with the assistance of an expert in mergers and consolidations. Each council selected its own timetable for completing the merger process, which included selecting a new CEO, restructuring the staff, and selling properties.

In addition, GSUSA reduced the size of its headquarters staff by 20 percent, modernized its program for girls, established a new brand identity, and embarked on a $1 billion fundraising campaign. Although membership dipped for a few years, it began growing again after the merger period concluded. Many of the newly merged councils also experienced increases in contributions and Girl Scout cookie revenue, enabling them to expand staffing and program opportunities for girls.

"This was a carefully planned, systematic, widely discussed, open, and—as far as humanly possible—democratic process," said a GSUSA senior executive. "All the study and research we did before embarking on it pointed to its necessity, and the results have done nothing but validate our decision.

"If you're leading this kind of change, you can gather information and advice until you're 99.999 percent sure you're doing the right thing," the executive continued, "but you'll never get to 100 percent. All you can do is think it through the best you can, make your decision, and jump."

Surprisingly, we found no distinction between proactive and reactive change among the associations studied. Our data confirm that no organization—regardless of how remarkable it is—can predict change with full accuracy and therefore be on target with its response in all instances. From time to time, all organizations are caught off guard and must react to unplanned events (such as the terrorist attacks on the United States on September 11, 2001).

The type of change is not as significant as how the organization responds to and learns from the change. Our data indicate that remarkable associations do not panic. Whether or not the change is anticipated, they maintain a clear understanding of their core purpose and willingly adapt how they do business to remain consistent with that purpose. They remain steadfast in their commitment to their members and their mission, often avoiding changes that have the potential to shift them away from that core, even if by doing so they sacrifice immediate payoffs.

Partnering for the Right Purpose

Measure 7: Alliance Building

Forming alliances with other organizations—whether nonprofit, for-profit, or government—ranked high on the priority list for both the study and comparison associations. Most of them had built several alliances that proved effective in generating revenue, raising awareness around a key issue, or building their organizational brand.

Where the two research groups differ is how they approach the seventh measure, alliance building. Associations in the study group pursue alliances that relate to existing strategies or that form a tight fit with their mission and purpose. In that regard, they determine with whom *not* to partner as much as with whom they should partner.

While remarkable associations are willing to admit they can't do everything on their own, they bring self-confidence to their alliance-building activities. Secure in who they are and what they bring to the table, these associations communicate clear expectations for each specific partnership and do not hesitate to walk away if a win-win situation does not materialize. But they're also willing to admit what they can't do on their own.

AARP, for example, aggressively searches for other organizations that have the expertise, skills, credibility, contacts, and other resources that complement or augment its own resources. In one year alone, AARP partnered with organizations as diverse as:

- Consumer Reports Health, to create an online tool that enables AARP members to easily compare the safety, effectiveness, and cost of prescription drugs.

- The Walgreens drug store chain, to administer millions of free health screenings— including cholesterol levels, blood pressure, bone density, and glucose levels—primarily in underserved communities.

- Chase Card Services, to sponsor Create the Good, a campaign and online resource aimed at raising awareness about social responsibility and community service.

- The NFL Players Association, to sponsor a community-based education initiative that pairs college-bound students and their families with NFL player mentors.

- SHRM, another remarkable association, to conduct a survey on the strategic implications of the aging U.S. workforce.

These represent just a few of AARP's many collaborations. For AARP, alliance building is all about fulfilling its mission of "enhancing the quality of life for all as we age, leading positive social change, and delivering value to members through information, advocacy and service."

NACo views partnerships as one means of offering valuable programs or services to cash-strapped counties without increasing its own staff. That's why it partnered with a technology company and an organization of public health officials to launch the Network of Care, an internet-based service that citizens can access to find specialized healthcare resources within a particular county. The association also teamed up with Microsoft and IBM to sponsor county-based pilot projects related to cloud computing, in addition to partnering with CVS/Caremark pharmacies to provide a prescription drug discount card that's free to residents of participating counties. In the latter case, NACo originally considered offering the discount card as a for-profit enterprise but decided it had greater value to counties as a benefit of membership.

In contrast, one comparison association typically approaches alliances as a means of paying the bills (corporate sponsorships) rather than as an opportunity to expand mission-based programming. Not surprisingly, the comparison association has far fewer alliances.

The American Dental Association (ADA) saw a need among its members for more sophisticated practice-management knowledge. Recognizing its limitations in that area, ADA turned to Northwestern University's Kellogg School of Management to develop a mini-MBA program specifically for dentists.

In that same vein, NACo collaborates with the graduate school of public policy at George Washington University to offer a county leadership institute. NACo asks state associations to identify up-and-coming leaders to participate in the four-day program. Corporate partners who underwrite portions of the program benefit from added visibility with this constituency.

ADA also sees the potential for collaboration with its competitors at state and local levels. It invested in the development of the

Tripartite System, a software package for managing and sharing membership data across a common platform. More than 60 state and local dental societies use the system to support membership billing, patient referrals, information retrieval, mailing list management, and grassroots lobbying efforts.

***

FINDING THE COMMON GROUND

It's not unusual for the National Association of Counties (NACo) to collaborate with several dozen organizations each year. One collaboration dates to the 1980s, when NACo and six associations with similar interests and overlapping issues—including the U.S. Conference of Mayors and the National League of Cities—formed The Big 7.

NACo considers several of The Big 7 as competition for some of its products and services. But any competition takes a back seat when representatives of The Big 7 meet monthly. They discuss hot issues and emerging trends and identify opportunities for working together and potentially pooling resources to advance a common cause. Every two years, the chair of the group rotates among the seven associations.

Whether forging alliances or remaking themselves, remarkable associations do not stray from clearly stated goals. What's more, they maintain a disciplined process to achieve those goals. Their counterparts in the comparison group are more likely to seize on opportunities that offer the potential for short-term gain. In general, the comparison associations seem less concerned about the long-term implications of their actions.

CHAPTER 5

Old Saws and Fresh Cuts

I N WHAT ways, if any, do the study's findings challenge the conventional wisdom?

That question, which Jim Collins posed to the Measures of Success Task Force, proved as intriguing as identifying the seven factors that distinguish remarkable associations from the rest of the pack.

To answer the question, we needed to identify what constituted conventional wisdom within the field of association management. First individually, then as a group, the task force compiled a list of widely held beliefs prevalent in the profession. Next we systematically compared the findings to conventional wisdom, acknowledging that it is far easier to disprove something than to prove it.

For example, consider this statement: "All apples are red." While proving this would pose quite a challenge, disproving it would not: You'd simply have to find one yellow apple.

In some instances, we easily picked out the yellow apples—the remarkable associations that did not adhere to conventional wisdom yet consistently flourished. The following are the conventional beliefs *not* supported by this study:

The smaller the board, the better. Were this conventional wisdom true, we should have seen smaller boards among the study group and larger boards in the comparison group. This was not the case. In fact, in one instance, a study association *added* two seats to its board, following a governance review.

Within the study group, board size ranged from eight (Radiological Society of North America) to 129 (National Association of Counties). The size of NACo's board does not hinder the organization's efficiency, speed of action, or ability to maintain focus on its mission. Study organizations with larger boards (more than 20 members) developed systems and structures that disperse power and decision-making authority.

Our data indicate board size isn't a significant factor in the effectiveness of the organization. What *does* matter is how boards and staff understand and align their roles. In general, boards in the study organizations were more strategic than operational. Similarly, study organizations were committed to collecting and analyzing data, which likely facilitated strategic decision making.

Board members should be selected via a democratic process. Many associations view elections as a reflection of democratic culture and values. Several organizations in both the study and comparison groups used the "any member can run for the board" approach, complete with candidate campaigning and speech-making.

Others relied on a nominating committee to select an essentially uncontested slate with one candidate for each open position. Two out of the nine associations in the study group use a competency model in which board candidates are selected based upon their skills, knowledge, and experience; one of those associations has even considered hiring a search firm to identify viable candidates.

PUT TO THE TEST

The Measures of Success Task Force compiled these statements of conventional wisdom within the association management profession, then tested them against the data gathered in the matched-pair research study.

1. One person should be at the top.
2. Keep 50 percent of annual expenses in reserves.
3. CEO should be an association professional.
4. CEO should come from outside the organization rather than within.
5. Don't get too far ahead of the membership.
6. Elections should reflect the democratic process.
7. Elected leaders should move through the ranks.
8. Small boards are better than big boards.
9. Organizations should be more member-driven than staff-driven.
10. Be innovative/on the cutting edge.
11. Run the association like a corporation.
12. Engage in consensus decision making.
13. Participatory management is best.
14. CEO should take a back seat to the elected leader.
15. CEO is always right.
16. Have a one-year term for elected leaders.
17. Association activities require constituent buy-in.
18. Radical times require radical change.
19. Proactive change is better than reactive change.
20. The board sets the policy; the staff implements it.
21. Staff should not be involved in selection of leaders.
22. CEO has no vote on the board.
23. Have a strategic plan.
24. A higher market share is better.

Although associations in the study group value previous leadership experience, none requires volunteers to follow a rigid, up-the-ladder approach to board service. Nor do these associations favor a particular selection or election process to populate their boards. Among these remarkable associations, however, there is a common denominator: They are highly effective in maintaining transparency and communicating how the process for identifying and recruiting capable, credible, and competent leaders works.

The CEO should be an association professional and come from outside the organization and its membership. The data do not support this assertion. Only three of the nine associations in the study group had followed this model when selecting the CEO in place during the Measures of Success project. Two associations had selected their CEO from within the membership, and four had chosen an internal candidate. Interestingly, two of the latter group had turned to the internal candidate after the short tenure of a CEO from the outside.

Similarly, the six remarkable associations that welcomed new CEOs between the first edition and revision of this book followed various paths to filling the top staff position. Two selected CEOs who had led other associations, two promoted internal candidates, one chose a new leader from among its membership, and one turned to the corporate sector for a new CEO.

Regardless of their background or how they came to the position, CEOs of remarkable associations typically had one trait in common: They matched themselves to the personality of the organization and understood what it expected of them.

Proactive change is better. Conventional wisdom would have us believe that remarkable associations take a proactive stance toward change, rather than a reactive one—yet that distinction did not emerge from the data. In fact, the type of change is not as significant as the response it evokes from the organization. Whether they initiate change themselves or react to change, remarkable associations do what it takes to remain committed to their core purpose. They not only learn from the change but also exhibit the will to take the action it requires of them.

Reserves should equal 50 percent of annual expenses. Study findings revise this statement upward. During the original research period, most associations in the study group maintained reserves of approximately 75 percent of their annual expenses. At least three of them had drawn on their reserves to invest in programs or organizational improvements to benefit members but still maintained a comfortable financial cushion.

Remarkable associations see "nonprofit" as a tax status, not a mental state. They understand that both for-profits and nonprofits make money; the difference lies in what is done with those profits. For-profit companies pay dividends to their shareholders, while nonprofits reinvest retained earnings into member programs and services.

WHO'S DRIVING?

Association executives are often asked to characterize their organizations as being either member-driven or staff-driven. Conventional wisdom says it's better to have volunteer leaders guide and remain in control of decision making (member-driven). Or, depending on whom you ask, some people argue that the best choice is to be "balanced-driven." In that model, neither staff nor members dominate decision making; decisions are reached through the cooperative efforts of both groups.

Our data do not indicate a relationship between decision-making models and organizational success. No one model predominates among the study or comparison groups. We found just as many member-driven associations among the comparison group as staff-driven associations among the study group. Some could also be described as balanced.

That said, the remarkable associations did differentiate themselves in a way that should put an end to the staff- versus member-driven debate. In short, the distinction doesn't matter. What *does* matter is being *data*-driven as well as *member-focused*.

Remarkable associations have a customer/member service orientation; continually gather and analyze data about members and the external environment; and use their mission, which is all about the members, as the touchstone for all activities. The member-focused, data-driven model produces the best possible scenario: Staff drives achievement, but both member leaders and the staff ultimately achieve success by maintaining a well-informed focus on the member.

Taking a for-profit company's perspective, members would be viewed as a market, triggering the question, "What can we sell to them?" Instead, remarkable associations view members as drivers, and the question becomes, "How can we serve them, and what do they need?"

Comparing the Findings

We initially decided to apply Collins' methodology to associations because we had confidence in the matched-pair approach. We suspected that many of his findings from the for-profit sector would apply equally well to the association environment, assuming they withstood the test of a full-fledged, comprehensive study.

Here's how the task force's findings compare with some of Collins' concepts from the for-profit sector.

Profit is one means of measuring success, not *the* means. *Good to Great* reveals that great for-profit companies do not focus on their profits as an end; they have other ways of measuring their ability to deliver on their value proposition.

The same holds true for associations. Remarkable associations consistently achieve a positive bottom line. They do so by steadfastly focusing on members' needs and ensuring that they deliver quality products and services to meet those needs. Comparison organizations more typically made decisions based primarily, if not solely, on profit. Ironically, they did not necessarily perform in the black consistently and often experienced a greater rate of member attrition.

Remarkable associations never disregard profit. Rather, they focus on carefully documenting member needs and then deliberately and consistently fulfilling those needs. Their healthy bottom line is a rewarding byproduct of their efforts.

Focus on the core, and experiment around the fringes. The behavior of remarkable associations fully supports this concept.

Remarkable associations never forget mission or members—why they were formed or who they serve—and are willing to undertake significant risks outside this core. In contrast, many organizations in the comparison group experienced changes that pulled them away from, or at least blurred, their mission.

Have a Big Hairy Audacious Goal (BHAG). Introduced in *Built to Last,* BHAG refers to a clear, compelling, and unifying focal point of effort for an organization. While remarkable associations had clearly stated goals and objectives, we did not find any evidence that they developed and pursued BHAGs. Their objectives flowed logically from their mission; as their mission remained constant, so, for the most part, did their objectives.

Foster a cultlike culture. Although the cultures of great companies are diverse, they share the characteristic of not accommodating the gadfly. Either people fit into the corporate mold or they move on.

Cultures of remarkable associations were typically described as "family-like" by those working within them; "cult-like" did not seem to apply. Remarkable associations have strong member-focused cultures. Staff members are never ambiguous about why they come to work each day: to serve the members. Moreover, they take pride and joy in doing so.

Exhibit Level 5 leadership. In *Good to Great,* Collins coined the expression "Level 5 Leader" to describe a CEO who exhibits personal humility as well as professional resolve. He found, much to his surprise, that great companies were led by people who were often socially shy, self-effacing, and reserved. Collins noted, "They are more like Lincoln and Socrates than Patton or Caesar."

We found that most associations, both study and comparison, had experienced their share of Pattons and Caesars during the study period and had thrived nonetheless. Given the wide range of leadership styles and personalities among CEOs past and present, we did not have evidence to suggest that Level 5 leaders are necessary for associations to function in a consistently remarkable way.

We did confirm that the study organizations were led by highly effective individuals who shared several characteristics. CEOs of remarkable associations understand the importance of including both members and staff in ongoing dialogues. Although they did not manage by consensus per se, they did ensure that they gathered input from a variety of sources before making decisions.

Moreover, these CEOs understood and were comfortable with their role as a steward—not owner—of the association. The association belongs to the members, so its vision must emanate from them, not from the CEO's corner office or from a small group of leaders.

Be a legislative leader. *Good to Great and the Social Sectors,* a monograph written by Jim Collins, advances the notion that CEOs in the for-profit sector have "executive" skills while those in the social sector have "legislative" skills. Specifically, the latter group relies on "persuasion, political currency, and shared interests to create conditions for the right decisions to happen."

Our research partially supports Collins' hypothesis. Corporate executives may be hired for their vision; CEOs of remarkable associations are hired to facilitate visionary thinking and to create a culture of possibilities. They are rarely, if ever, the sole decision maker; they must share that responsibility with volunteer leaders, who rely on input from members and the environment. The findings emphasize that association CEOs are brokers, not sole proprietors, of ideas.

Get the right people on the bus and the wrong people off. This concept poses a challenge for associations because they have two sets of passengers—staff and volunteers. CEOs can exert much more influence with the former group than with the latter. Several CEOs in the study group spoke about making staff changes to improve performance and morale, while acknowledging that they can inherit

THE RESULTS IN CONTEXT

Findings from the Measures of Success project, as well as the research findings of Jim Collins, are consistent with literature about learning organizations and systems. To use Collins' terminology, great organizations "build clocks rather than tell time." In other words, they build systems that effectively integrate inputs, processes, and outputs. Acting together, these various parts produce more than they could individually.

In *The Fifth Discipline Fieldbook* (1994, Doubleday), Peter M. Senge, Art Kleiner, Charlotte Roberts, Richard Ross, and Bryan Smith define a learning organization as one that transforms "experience into knowledge—accessible to the whole organization and relevant to its core purpose." Further, the authors observe that learning organizations:

Continuously test their experience. They compare what they think they know to the reality as derived from research.

Produce knowledge. In this context, knowledge means know-how. It is fundamentally different from information, which is data that knowledge transforms into effective action. The purpose of knowledge is not to merely inform but to change behavior.

Share knowledge. Knowledge is accessible to individuals throughout the organization.

Make learning relevant. Learning organizations gather knowledge that helps them forward their mission. They purposely focus on their core mission and don't become distracted by information overload.

These characteristics describe remarkable organizations as well. The Measures of Success study revealed that disciplined organizations transform information they experience into knowledge (know-how) they can use to further their mission. They are on a constant quest for improvement.

---

volunteer leaders who make it challenging to forge effective partnerships between staff and volunteers.

Develop a "stop doing" list. *Good to Great* emphasizes that great organizations exercise the discipline to simply stop engaging in unproductive or inefficient activities. Likewise, remarkable associations maintain clear goals and have a disciplined process to evaluate how well their products and services remain aligned with their mission and members' documented needs. When a program or service no longer fits, these associations terminate it to make room for something better.

A number of our findings are consistent with those identified by Collins. Several findings unique to the association environment are also evident. First, remarkable associations are intensely data-driven. They rarely miss an opportunity to solicit feedback, gather opinions, and collect statistics, all of which they analyze and act on. A second unique finding was the commitment by remarkable associations to ongoing dialogue and engagement, both among and between staff and volunteers.

The concept of collaborating for the right purpose does not have a counterpart in the corporate world. Unlike for-profit companies that engage in intense competition, associations seek to achieve their goals through cooperation, even if their collaborators pose competition in some areas. Few associations have the resources to accomplish all their goals on their own, so they must work with others in pursuit of fulfilling their mission.

The Road to Remarkable

In their own right, the seven measures of success are not ground-breaking concepts. After all, many associations form alliances and foster dialogue among and with their staff and members.

Taken together, however, the seven measures overlap and interact in so many ways that they weave a pattern of long-term success for the associations that employ the measures to their fullest potential.

What truly distinguished associations in the study group was their performance relative to the seven measures: They exhibited the measures consistently and continually, integrating all seven into the way they did business and into their very culture.

Remarkable associations find it second nature to deliver stellar customer service; develop products, services, and alliances that support their mission and purpose; gather and analyze member data; and make the adaptations or clear-cut changes that enable them to continue fulfilling their mission to serve members. One measure feeds into another and yet another, as illustrated below.

Input and Output Framework

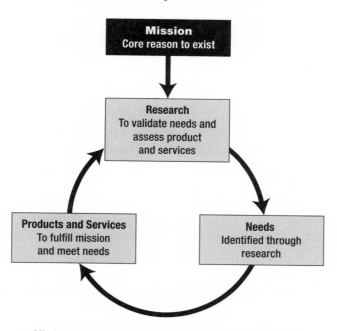

Mission drives research that reveals specific needs. The needs determine program, product, and service development, which are further evaluated to determine value.

Mission is subdivided into specific needs—identified through research—resulting in the development of products and services, which are then subjected to further research to ascertain what is working and what needs to change.

When we looked at the mountains of printed material, pages of statistics, and transcripts of personal interviews, several general themes emerged. Overall, we observed that:

- **Members and mission are at the heart of remarkable associations—and member value is the blood that keeps the heart pumping.** While seeking to build and maintain a strong relationship with their members, remarkable organizations never stop being inquisitive about how they can refine and enhance the value they provide.

- **Remarkable associations deliver.** They continually research member needs; relate those needs to the mission; and then develop, adapt, and refine products and services. They always look for the best solutions to provide valuable resources and services.

- **All organizations must deal with setbacks, failures, and crises, but not all of them learn from these events.** The remarkable organizations don't become frozen in place or time. They acknowledge their failures, learn from their experiences, make changes or adaptations, and move on.

    We also noted these specific behaviors, which build on and add nuance to the seven measures outlined in Chapters 2, 3, and 4.

REMARKABLE ASSOCIATIONS...	GOOD ASSOCIATIONS OFTEN...
Have confidence in who they are and are well on the way to determining—or already know—who they want to be.	May still be struggling with who they are and have given little serious thought to who they want to be.
Ask what members need.	Decide what members need.
Do what needs to be done.	Talk about what needs to be done.
Have learned to let go of programs and services that no longer serve or resonate with members.	Continue to hang on to what may have worked in the past but may now be irrelevant.
Embrace product failures as an opportunity to learn how to better serve members; look for ways to re-use or repackage what failed.	View failures almost as embarrassments, as something not to revisit or even recall.

REMARKABLE ASSOCIATIONS...	GOOD ASSOCIATIONS OFTEN...
Enjoy camaraderie within an open, sharing environment where a sense of single purpose prevails. ("We're all in this together.")	May have a sense of teamwork within departments but usually not across the entire organization, leading to a silo mentality. ("That's not my job.")
Question the status quo.	Protect the status quo.
Are methodical and disciplined about collecting member data and opinions.	Take a random, inconsistent approach to gathering member data.
Use data vertically and horizontally, enabling data to permeate the organization.	Use data vertically (usually a top-down approach).
Do their homework, through surveys, assessments, and evaluations, before launching or discontinuing a product or service.	Rely more on intuition, assumptions, and chance to guide product development and improvement.
Exhibit a "What if...?" mentality when confronting challenges.	Exhibit a "Yes, but..." mentality when challenges arise.
Remain attuned to the external environment, particularly the competition.	Do not engage in much scanning of the external environment, relying instead on organizational leaders to provide a view of the world.
Strive to understand what precipitated a crisis and face it head-on.	Make excuses or place blame when a crisis arises, often becoming immobilized by it.
Talk *with* members at every opportunity.	Talk *to* members, both in face-to-face and other types of communication.

One might be tempted to point to the list of associations in the study group and say, "Well, of course they can afford to do that because they have money, or clout, or _____ (fill in the blank)." The fact is, all of the remarkable associations have, at times during the study period, operated with severely limiting factors, including a large deficit, a serious IRS challenge, a sizeable decline in membership, the sudden death of a CEO, and a crisis within the members' profession. Associations in the comparison group became paralyzed by such circumstances, often for years. They obsessed on their limitations and sought excuses for their inaction or inability to capitalize on opportunities.

CEO CONFIDENTIAL

Data from the Measures of Success project could not prove exactly what is required to become a remarkable association. But the data did reveal some practices that distinguish remarkable associations from their good counterparts.

If an association follows these practices, it will increase the probability that it, too, will become remarkable:

- **Keep your eyes and your minds wide open.** Products and services should emanate from two sources: your mission and your members' documented needs.
- **Develop and foster a strong customer service culture.** Keeping members front and center is everyone's job.
- **Keep your balance.** Remain firm about the *what*—your mission—and flexible about the *how*—your products and services.
- **Clean your plate.** As you add new programs and services, eliminate those that no longer serve a need. Have only one sacred cow—your mission.
- **Seek to influence, not control.** The CEO's job is to facilitate visionary thinking and be a broker of ideas, not to force others to adopt his or her vision.
- **Remain humble.** You don't know it all. The best source of what members need is the membership itself. Seek out members' views often and in a variety of ways.
- **Be a good neighbor.** Initiate and foster relationships with organizations that may not share your overall mission but do share your desire to accomplish certain goals. Don't make friends for the sake of appearances or profits—do it for the sake of your mission.

In contrast, the remarkable associations not only recognize but also accept their limiting factors. Embracing the culture of opportunity as presented to them, they proceed to operate and accomplish their mission undeterred.

CHAPTER 6

Putting the 7 Measures to Work

W HILE READING about the attributes of remarkable associa- tions, you may have made a mental assessment of your own association's inclinations. For example, you might have thought, "Would we react with the same speed and agility to an organizational crisis?" or wondered, "Do our products and services truly line up with our mission?"

The process through which such questions are answered will be as unique as the association asking them. With that in mind, here are summaries of how three organizations of varying age, size, and structure have incorporated the seven measures into their cultures and operations. (For additional ideas to implement in your associa- tion, see Appendix E: How to Measure the Measures.)

Associated Builders and Contractors (ABC)

This 70,000-member federation participated in the Measures of Success study but wasn't selected as a remarkable association. More than a little disappointed by being placed in the group of comparison associations, ABC's staff members and volunteer leaders delved into the study's results. All employees and members of the executive committee read *7 Measures of Success* and participated in book-club discussion groups; joined by numerous chapter presidents, this group also completed an online survey of the areas where they thought ABC could easily make progress. Interestingly, staff members and volunteers had divergent opinions. The latter group selected a customer service culture (Measure 1) as most likely to yield improvements quickly, while staff answers were equally distributed among all seven measures.

With the survey results as a starting point, ABC hosted a one-day, facilitated brainstorming session that addressed four questions:

- What does ABC do well in this area?
- What could ABC do better?
- How can ABC measure progress?
- What might ABC need to improve competency in this area?

Following another one-day brainstorming session with chapter presidents and a two-day executive committee meeting, all dedicated to analyzing ABC's performance relative to the seven measures, the association's leadership finalized a plan.

For starters, the group decided to rewrite ABC's mission statement as a precursor to better aligning its products and services with the mission (Measure 2). Conversations among staff vice presidents revealed the need to boost dialogue and engagement with internal audiences (Measure 4) and to redesign the national database to better capture and use information gathered from the field (Measure 3). Perhaps the most significant change related to the CEO being a broker of ideas (Measure 5): The executive committee voted to restructure the staff by adding the new position of chief operating officer (COO), thus freeing up more time the CEO could dedicate to building and strengthening alliances (Measure 7).

INGRAINED IN THE CULTURE

True to their demonstrated commitment to action, organizations within the study group did not remain content with past performance. To retain their noteworthy staff, programs, operations, financial situation, and organizational flexibility—and, more important, improve them—the majority of the nine associations put the seven measures to use in numerous ways. For example:

- The National Association of Counties (NACo) reviewed results of the Measures of Success study with its entire staff and 130-member board, then asked each group for a candid analysis of how the association actually performed relative to each measure. While customer service (Measure 1) rated highly, for example, the general consensus was that the association came up short on using data-driven strategies (Measure 3). One management retreat tackled the same topic in more depth, with senior staff confirming that data-driven strategies offered the most room for improvement. Consequently, NACo began surveying its members more frequently and partnered with some private organizations to gather more data on the counties NACo serves. Based on members' input, NACo expanded its educational programming to include more webinars and increased the for-profit services and products it offers.

- For Associated General Contractors (AGC), the seven measures served as a foundation for one of its annual reports. The report demonstrated how, in the preceding year, the association had lived up to each measure. Organizational adaptability (Measure 6) became a priority when membership dipped during the 2008-09 recession; one of AGC's moves was to transform its traditional committee structure into special interest forums. The forum structure offers a less expensive means of information sharing and participation for employees of member firms that can't financially justify attending an AGC convention or committee meeting.

- At their orientation session, new board members of the Ohio Society of CPAs (OSCPA) receive copies of *7 Measures of Success* and the annual *Volunteer Leadership Issue* of *Associations Now* to help explain their duties and clarify their expectations. The measures are reviewed and reinforced frequently among staff members as well. They view the seven measures as best practices and often incorporate the measures terminology into their discussions—saying, for example, "We really don't have enough data yet to make a solid business case for that decision."

"*7 Measures* did not give us any answers. Rather, it gave us a way to think about the right questions to ask," observed Kirk Pickerel, CAE, who retired in 2011 as president and CEO of ABC.

International Association of Administrative Professionals (IAAP)

Don Bretthauer, CAE, admitted being a bit skeptical when *7 Measures* first appeared on the scene. As IAAP's executive director at the time, he had seen numerous approaches to nonprofit management come and go—but he liked the book's research-based observations and thought they might help IAAP's staff and leaders guide the 25,000-member association through a somewhat tumultuous period in its more than 50-year history.

First, IAAP's leadership looked at the mission statement and decided the long, nebulous description didn't accurately reflect the association's true identity. The board drafted five new mission statements and polled the membership to narrow the choices. After some tweaking, the two finalists were again presented to the members, who favored this concise mission statement: Enhancing the success of career-minded administrative professionals by providing opportunities for growth through education, community building, and leadership development.

"That was our first effort at getting data and promoting dialogue and engagement," Bretthauer said. "We wanted the members to have buy-in on the new mission statement, so they'd be more aware of what the organization was doing." IAAP also started surveying its members about their attitudes, gathering different information than it had in the past.

With the new mission statement and data in hand, board and staff began "mission testing"—comparing programs, products, and services to IAAP's professed purpose. Not all activities passed the test, leading IAAP to phase out some long-time activities. For example, for years the association had tracked Continuing Education Units (CEUs) on its members' behalf and issued certificates to them. Yet few members used the service, which other organizations in the profession also offered. "Serving as a repository of people's attendance at meetings was a convenience for our members, but it didn't align with our mission statement," Bretthauer explained. "We just stopped doing it, so we'd have more time to devote to another opportunity that would have greater impact for our members."

For IAAP, the next logical step was to incorporate the seven measures into its strategic planning. The association created its Executive Oversight Committee, consisting of three elected officers, the executive director, and a staff member to serve as project manager. Committee members outlined the areas in which they wanted to see the association improve, then appointed short-term action teams—with both staff and volunteer members—to help bring the changes to fruition. This process has continued; each spring, the Executive Oversight Committee reviews the previous year's progress, identifies new areas for improvement, and appoints new action teams. One team, for example, analyzed the association's alliances in the preceding five years, using the results to develop a standardized process for evaluating potential partners in the future.

Another team's work led to a significant change in one of IAAP's signature programs. In 2011, IAAP restructured its certification program—which traditionally had offered two credentials—to support one general credential that can be expanded upon with specialties. After earning the new Certified Administrative Professional (CAP) designation, for example, a member might take additional exams related to specialties such as organizational management, medical or insurance administration, or technology/software. The change simplified the certification program while also providing numerous ways to expand it to reflect members' specialized skills.

The extent to which the seven measures have become ingrained in the association's culture might best be described by the theme IAAP's 2011–12 international president selected to guide her year in office: "Making the Leap to Remarkable." When introducing the theme to IAAP's members, the international president noted, "The Leap to Remarkable isn't a destination—it's a journey. This [theme] encapsulates the vision that our association has been working toward."

Bretthauer observed, "We use the seven measures to do incremental improvements. Our process is a hybrid between business planning and long-term strategic planning, and it keeps everyone focused on improving the organization." In particular, staff appreciate the association's continued focus on data-driven strategies (Measure 3) because they feel confident about making difficult decisions that are fully supported by usage statistics and survey results.

On his own, Bretthauer tackled the idea of the CEO as a broker of ideas (Measure 5). For six months, he tracked how he spent his time each day—and discovered he typically dealt with so many internal issues that he rarely got around to reviewing ideas from outside the organization and offering creative options to the board. That realization led to a staff restructuring, which changed reporting relationships for some of Bretthauer's direct reports.

He added, "There isn't any prescription for how you should use the seven measures. They don't offer a cookie-cutter model but rather provide a framework for change, one that can be adapted to your association and how it works."

American Academy of Hospice and Palliative Medicine (AAHPM)

Founded in 1998, AAHPM had reached a critical juncture when the Measures of Success project concluded with publication of *7 Measures of Success*. With membership increasing steadily—and physician members preparing for board certification for the first time—AAHPM had begun the transition to a leadership-oriented board, rather than one that sometimes dabbled in operational issues. The seven measures provided a perfect framework for managing the growth and taking the 4,000-member association to the next level.

"The book reintroduced to some volunteer leaders the notion that association management is really a business, so it helps legitimize the profession. They realized that there are resources, theories, and practices that go into making an association successful," said Steve Smith, CAE, AAHPM's executive director/CEO.

After reading *7 Measures,* the 18-member board and the 10-person staff began incorporating the book's terminology into trainings, discussions, and decision making. When a decision looms on the horizon, for example, the association's leaders remind themselves to first engage in data gathering and dialogue before beginning any deliberations that will lead to decision making. AAHPM also introduced the seven measures to its five strategic coordinating committees—one for each of its strategic goals—and to the task forces that focus on various activities which support those goals.

"We worked hard to get our entire governance structure working through the same process of data-driven strategies and dialogue and engagement. That has created trust and helped the board become more strategic," Smith explained. Board members became less focused on the details of implementing a particular initiative because they trusted the task force proposing it had gathered supporting data and member feedback. In turn, task force members felt more empowered because the board relied on them for strategic recommendations.

7 Measures doesn't tell an association specifically what to do, added Smith, but it provides inspiration. For example:

- AAHPM dedicated one staff retreat to discussing a customer service culture (Measure 1). With the assistance of a facilitator, staff members generated guidelines for good service to influence every interaction with members, either in person or on the phone. As a constant reminder to implement the guidelines, not tuck them away in a written document, the association gave employees coffee mugs bearing its stated commitment to customer service.

- In support of both data-driven strategies and dialogue and engagement (Measures 3 and 4), the association seeks input from its members every month. The research might range from a quick online or phone survey, to formalized focus groups, to a full-blown member satisfaction or market research study. The results have helped AAHPM identify critical transition points for its members—such as completing a residency, starting a practice, or serving as a mentor—and provide appropriate information and programs to support them at those times. Also, based on the feedback it received from members, AAHPM made an early move into social media; its annual meeting routinely produces a high volume of traffic on Twitter as attendees share content and comments from sessions.

- In addition to partnering with an association of nurses to host its annual conference, AAHPM dedicates a certain percentage of staff time to external outreach and alliance building (Measure 7). The association aims to increase collaboration with other medical specialties, in support of its purpose to improve the care of patients with life-threatening or serious conditions.

"Many small associations use their size as a barrier; they assume they can't do something because they lack the resources," noted Smith. "We take the opposite approach—we assume we can do anything because we are nimble. And if we align everything we do with our mission and strategic goals, and the membership provides validation through dialogue and engagement, why wouldn't we do it?"

Profiles of Remarkable Associations

Following are organizational snapshots, updated in late 2011, of the nine associations that formed the study group.

AARP

Headquarters: Washington, DC

Founded: 1958 (as the American Association of Retired Persons); AARP is the official name of the organization, not an abbreviation.

Nature: 501(c)(4)

Scope: National

Members: 40 million

Chapters: 2,400

Employees: 2,218

Board: 22

Annual Budget: $800 million

CEO: A. Barry Rand, chief executive officer

Website: www.aarp.org

Vision: A society in which everyone lives their life with dignity and purpose, and in which AARP helps people fulfill their goals and dreams.

Mission: AARP's mission is to enhance the quality of life for all as we age, leading positive social change, and delivering value to members through information, advocacy, and service.

Guiding Principles

- Collective purpose
- Collective voice
- Collective purchasing power

American College of Cardiology

Headquarters: Washington, DC

Founded: 1949

Nature: 501(c)(3), professional

Scope: International

Members: 40,000

Chapters: 49

Employees: 350

Board: 31

Annual Budget: $100 million

CEO: Jack Lewin, M.D., chief executive officer

Website: www.cardiosource.org

Mission: The mission of the American College of Cardiology is to advocate for quality cardiovascular care—through education, research promotion, development and application of standards and guidelines—and to influence health care policy.

Core Values:

- *Professionalism*: The interests of patients are primary.

- *Knowledge*: The College must promote growth, dissemination, and application of knowledge about cardiovascular medicine.

- *Value of the cardiovascular specialist*: The cardiovascular profession makes a distinct contribution to medical care that should be recognized and enhanced.

- *Integrity*: Honesty, compliance with legal requirements, and ethical behavior are essential in all activities.

- *Member driven*: The College and its major activities must be led by active members and must promote volunteerism.

- *Inclusiveness*: The College involves a broad range of volunteers that reflects the composition of its membership.

American Dental Association

Headquarters: Chicago, Illinois

Founded: 1859

Nature: 501(c)(6), professional

Scope: National

Members: 157,000

Chapters: 598

Employees: 400

Board: 17 members, 7 officers

Annual Budget: $116 million

CEO: Kathleen O'Loughlin, D.M.D., executive director and chief operating officer

Website: www.ada.org

Vision: To be the recognized leader on oral health.

Mission: The American Dental Association (ADA) is the professional association of dentists that fosters the success of a diverse membership and advances the oral health of the public.

Associated General Contractors of America

Headquarters:	Arlington, Virginia
Founded:	1918
Nature:	501(c)(6), trade
Scope:	National
Members:	33,000
Chapters:	95
Employees:	65
Board:	24
Annual Budget:	$18 million
CEO:	Stephen E. Sandherr, chief executive officer
Website:	www.agc.org

Vision: American General Contractors of America's (AGC's) vision is to promote a better industry for the professionals who build America's future.

Mission: AGC serves our nation's construction professionals by promoting the skill, integrity, and responsibility of those who build America.

Girl Scouts of the USA

Headquarters: New York, New York

Founded: 1912

Nature: 501(c)(3), individual membership

Scope: National

Members: 3.2 million

Chapters: 112

Employees: 315

Board: 30 (7-member Executive Committee)

Annual Budget: $61 million

CEO: Anna Maria Chávez, chief executive officer

Website: www.girlscouts.org

Vision: To be the premier leadership organization for girls.

Mission: Girl Scouting builds girls of courage, confidence, and character, who make the world a better place.

Purpose: The purpose of Girl Scouts is inspiring girls with the highest ideals of character, conduct, patriotism, and service so that they may become happy and resourceful citizens.

National Association of Counties

Headquarters: Washington, DC

Founded: 1935

Nature: 501(c)(4), trade

Scope: National

Members: 3,007

Employees: 79

Board: 129 (4 Officers)

Annual Budget: $20 million

CEO: Larry E. Naake, executive director

Website: www.naco.org

Vision: The National Association of Counties (NACo) vision is to be an effective voice for America's counties in our nation's capitol and to support counties and county officials in their efforts to provide improved programs and services to their residents.

Mission: NACo is a full-service organization that provides an extensive line of services including legislative, research, and technical, as well as public affairs assistance to its members. The association acts as a liaison with other levels of government, works to improve public understanding of counties, serves as a national advocate for counties, and provides them with resources to help them find innovative methods to meet the challenges they face.

Ohio Society of Certified Public Accountants

Headquarters: Dublin, Ohio

Founded: 1908

Nature: 501(c)(6), professional

Scope: State

Members: 22,000

Employees: 54

Board: 17

Annual Budget: $10 million

CEO: J. Clarke Price, CAE, president

Website: www.ohioscpa.com

Core Purpose: CPAs...Making sense of a changing and complex world.

Vision: CPAs are the trusted professionals who enable people and organizations to shape their future. Combining insight with integrity, CPAs deliver value by

- Communicating the total picture with clarity and objectivity;
- Translating complex information into critical knowledge;
- Anticipating and creating opportunities; and
- Designing pathways that transform vision into reality.

Mission: The Ohio Society of Certified Public Accountants represents the interests of its members—whether in public practice, corporate practice, government, or education—and supports members in fulfilling their responsibility to serve the public interest.

Radiological Society of North America

Headquarters:	Oak Brook, Illinois
Founded:	1915
Nature:	501(c)(3), professional
Scope:	International
Members:	46,000
Employees:	180
Board:	8
Annual Budget:	$45 million
CEO:	Mark G. Watson, executive director
Website:	www.rsna.org

Vision: The Radiological Society of North America (RSNA) aspires to be the premier professional association dedicated to patient care through science and education in radiology.

Mission: The RSNA promotes excellence in patient care and health care delivery through education, research, and technologic innovation.

Core Values:
- Integrity
- Excellence
- Professionalism
- Leadership
- Innovation
- Service
- Volunteerism

Society for Human Resource Management

Headquarters: Alexandria, Virginia

Founded: 1948 (as the American Society for Personnel Administration)

Nature: 501(c)(6), professional

Scope: International

Members: 250,000

Chapters: 575

Employees: 339

Board: 11

Annual Budget: $112 million

CEO: Henry Jackson, president and chief executive officer

Website: www.shrm.org

Vision: The Society for Human Resource Management (SHRM) will be a globally recognized authority whose voice is heard on the most pressing people management issues of the day—now and in the future.

Mission: SHRM is the global HR organization that exists to:

- Build and sustain partnerships with human resource professionals, media, governments, non-governmental organizations, businesses and academic institutions to address people management challenges that influence the effectiveness and sustainability of their organizations and communities.

- Provide a community for human resource professionals, media, governments, non-governmental organizations, businesses and academic institutions to share expertise and create innovative solutions on people management issues.

- Proactively provide thought leadership, education, and research to human resource professionals, media, governments, non-governmental organizations, businesses, and academic institutions.

- Serve as an advocate to ensure that policy makers, law makers, and regulators are aware of key people concerns facing organizations and the human resource profession.

Financial Ratio Comparisons

The tables on the following pages offer a financial snapshot of all the organizations within the study and comparison groups. Please note that the data are all from 2002, the year for which the most complete data were available at the time the first edition was published.

RATIO	❶ RESERVES: TOTAL EXPENSE	❷ NET REVENUE: TOTAL EXPENSE	❸ DUES REVENUE: TOTAL REVENUE	❹ DUES REVENUE: TOTAL MEMBERS	❺ TOTAL REVENUE: TOTAL STAFF	❻ TOTAL EXPENSE: TOTAL STAFF	❼ NON-DUES REVENUE: TOTAL STAFF
Study Group 1	80.42%	-3.06%	7.79%	129	245,108	252,836	226,007
Comparison Group 1	23.01%	3.55%	33.00%	110	163,702	158,088	109,680
Study Group 2	116.55%	-16.27%	18.52%	288	198,586	237,166	161,803
Comparison Group 2	79.12%	-2.74%	24.02%	286	173,597	178,482	131,901
Study Group 3	119.59%	-3.70%	70.92%	277	215,147	223,422	62,575
Comparison Group 3	29.71%	7.37%	72.77%	431	159,728	148,765	43,497
Study Group 4	68.48%	13.08%	23.33%	1,838	223,947	197,471	171,707
Comparison Group 4	-6.94%	-1.62%	8.97%	38,873	148,319	150,763	135,020
Study Group 5	24.33%	1.75%	51.40%	157	155,304	152,630	75,478
Comparison Group 5	177.27%	7.37%	79.86%	102	141,934	132,196	28,591
Study Group 6	108.50%	14.84%	37.60%	152	301,175	262,261	187,931
Comparison Group 6	4.79%	-0.46%	13.33%	473	255,796	256,508	221,754
Study Group 7	84.43%	0.87%	52.28%	432	206,042	202,693	98,318
Comparison Group 7	22.29%	-16.52%	15.75%	173	178,959	214,367	150,768
Study Group 8	155.23%	-13.36%	39.44%	7	134,840	155,634	81,654
Comparison Group 8	79.47%	-7.75%	0%	0	144,166	156,281	144,166
Study Group 9	53.51%	33.15%	36.00%	1	16,793	12,612	7,558
Comparison Group 9	21.51%	0.25%	0%	0	223,968	223,406	221,832

RATIO	RESERVES: TOTAL EXPENSE	NET REVENUE: TOTAL EXPENSE	DUES REVENUE: TOTAL REVENUE	DUES REVENUE: TOTAL MEMBERS	TOTAL REVENUE: TOTAL STAFF	TOTAL EXPENSE: TOTAL STAFF	NON-DUES REVENUE: TOTAL STAFF
Average Study	90.12%	3.03%	37.48%	365	188,549	188,525	119,226
Average Comparison	47.80%	-1.17%	27.52%	4,494	176,685	179,873	131,912
Median Study	84.43%	0.87%	37.60%	157	206,042	202,693	98,318
Median Comparison	23.01%	-0.46%	15.75%	173	163,702	158,088	135,020

Notes on Data Columns

❶ Reserves = Unrestricted Net Assets (Balance Sheet)
Total Expense = Total Expenses (Statement of Activities)

❷ Net Revenue = Total Revenue less Total Expense less Unrealized Gains / (or plus Losses) on Investments (Statement of Activities)
Total Expense = Total Expenses (Statement of Activities)

❸ Dues Revenue = Total Revenue from all membership dues categories (Statement of Activities)
Total Revenue = Total Revenue less Unrealized Gains / (or plus Losses) on Investments (Statement of Activities)

❹ Dues Revenue = Total Revenue from all membership dues categories (Statement of Activities)
Members = Total dues paying members (or total members if that is all that is available) (Other Data)

❺ Total Revenue = Total Revenue less Unrealized Gains / (or plus Losses) on Investments (Statement of Activities)
Total Staff = Full Time Equivalents (Other Data)

❻ Total Expense = Total Expenses (Statement of Activities)
Total Staff = Full Time Equivalents (Other Data)

❼ Non-Dues Revenue = Total Revenue (see above) - Dues Revenue (see above)
Total Staff = Full Time Equivalents (Other Data)

Average Number of Years in the Red vs. Years in the Black: Study vs. Comparison Groups

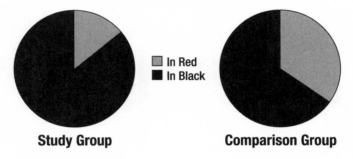

▢ In Red
■ In Black

Study Group   **Comparison Group**

Research Methodology, Timeline, and Tools

Research Methodology

The Measures of Success Task Force began its work in early 2003. First on the agenda was generating the list of great associations from which both the study and comparison groups would be drawn. In *Good to Great,* Jim Collins had used stock price to determine which companies made the cut for his study. This objective measure has no equivalent in the association sector. Therefore, the task force followed the jurying process that Collins and Jerry Porras had employed when researching *Built to Last.*

The American Society of Association Executives (ASAE) generated a random, nth-name sample of 1,000 CEOs, number-two executives, and industry leaders within its membership database. These executives received an explanatory letter and a request to nominate, in rank order, their choices for the top five associations in the country. Two follow-up mailings and a reminder postcard contributed to a response rate of 32 percent; this represents a 95 percent confidence level for sampling error.

The list generated by the survey respondents numbered 506 associations. The top 104 associations—those mentioned most frequently by respondents—received invitations to participate in the Measures of Success project, along with a request for preliminary data related to finances, membership, leadership, and organizing structure. Of the 51 associations that responded to this initial mailing (a 49 percent response rate), 82 percent indicated their interest in participating. Any association with a close connection to the project, such as a staff member serving on the task force, was disqualified from consideration.

While the survey was in progress, The Center for Association Leadership hired two full-time research investigators, both recent college graduates. Collins had suggested taking this approach to getting much of the work done because he has employed it himself. In Collins' view, recent graduates are accustomed to working hard and typically bring an active curiosity to digging through data to unearth nuggets of valuable information. In fact, he praised his research investigators for being "chimps"—a reference to Curious George, the fictitious character in children's storybooks, whose insatiable urge to discover more about the world led to many adventures.

Also with guidance from Collins, task force members developed criteria to apply to the potential participants and identified the period of study as the 15 years preceding and including 2003. The criteria were selected to reduce the likelihood that any findings of the study could be attributed to a particular characteristic or circumstance, such as a CEO with tenure over the entire span of the study, or an anomaly, such as an economic downturn within the association's trade or profession.

To be eligible for consideration for either the study or comparison groups an association needed to have:

- Been in operation for at least 20 years;
- Finished more years in the black than in the red;
- Exhibited the ability to retain members, donors, or market share during the study period; and
- Had more than one CEO during the study period.

In addition to meeting these criteria, an association had to be willing to fully cooperate in the research process. That meant providing detailed, often confidential, financial and membership information; submitting reams of paper, including publications, annual reports, and meeting minutes; hosting site visits; and answering numerous questions about its policies, procedures, and internal operations.

This cooperation on the part of the research subjects marks one area of departure from Collins' work. Where he had access to public documents detailing financial performance, for example, the task force relied on the associations' cooperation to provide the data. Collins conducted his research with the full awareness, if not the cooperation, of the companies being studied; the Measures of Success Task Force needed associations to provide both.

Another limitation to participation was an association's ability to provide the appropriate data. Several associations, despite their desire to participate, had to withdraw from the study because they either did not have the staff resources necessary to generate all the data requested or did not have complete data for the full study period. Other groups were excused from the study because the task force was unable to find suitable associations to form a matched pair.

Making the Lists

Once the research investigators had gathered preliminary data for review, the task force began the process of selecting which organizations to study in depth. The intent was to include all types of organizations (trade, professional, philanthropic), reflect various geographic scopes (state, national, international), and represent various membership sizes (small, medium, large).

Several associations immediately stood out as having performed consistently in the black and having maintained a consistent member/donor base during the study period; in addition, all had received frequent mentions by the ASAE members who participated in the jurying process. These became candidates for the study group of remarkable associations.

Ultimately, the study group was composed of these nine organizations (see Appendix A for organizational profiles):

- AARP
- American College of Cardiology
- American Dental Association
- Associated General Contractors of America
- Girl Scouts of the USA
- National Association of Counties
- Ohio Society of Certified Public Accountants
- Radiological Society of North America
- Society for Human Resource Management

To identify suitable candidates for the comparison group, the task force looked for associations that were similar to the study group in terms of budget and staff size, type (such as individual membership organization), and geographic scope. Whenever possible, efforts were made to match organizations that had similar missions or served similar memberships.

For the most part, the task force selected the nine members of the comparison group from the list of 105 organizations generated by the jurying process. In two instances, the task force cast its net wider to locate a better match for a study group.

The major differences between the study and comparison groups rested with their respective performances on the selection criteria, primarily those related to financial health and membership retention. In other words, associations in the comparison group were similar in all major respects to their counterparts in the study group, except that they had experienced fewer years in the black and/or had higher membership attrition rates.

All the associations studied—no matter which group they were placed in—were strong performers. The aim of the Measures of Success project was to compare remarkable and good associations, not good and bad ones. The project's value lies in discerning the often subtle differences between two well-matched organizations—what one association did or didn't do to give it a performance or financial edge on its counterpart.

Data Gathering and Analysis

Having placed 18 organizations into nine matched pairs, the task force outlined the areas for comparison and analysis. Once again drawing on the methodology employed by Collins and Porras in *Built to Last*, the task force selected 11 variables to identify differences among groups:

1. Vision (core values, mission, purpose, goals)
2. Markets, Competitors, and the Environment
3. Organizational Arrangements (structure, policies, systems)
4. Use of Technology
5. Business Strategy
6. Products and Services
7. Leadership (staff, elected)
8. Community and Culture
9. Financial Health
10. Physical Setting and Location
11. Public Policy

The Center for Association Leadership partnered with a specialist in behavioral research who guided the development of both a process and a set of tools that included multiple data inputs, in multiple formats. We structured the process and the instruments together. This ensured they were consistent in focus and could be related to one another, with the variables serving as a least common denominator, even though the nature of the information differed (structured, quantitative versus open-ended, qualitative).

In both design and implementation, we adhered to a high professional standard for conducting behavioral research that involves collecting data of multiple types, through multiple media, then testing them against the hypotheses developed at the outset. In other words, we tested to see which variables were most closely associated with sustained, outstanding organizational performance.

The task force employed the following process:

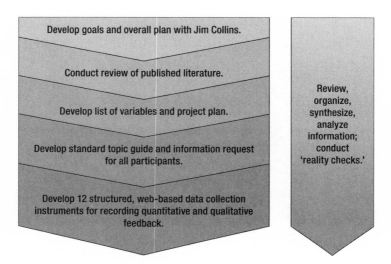

Develop goals and overall plan with Jim Collins.

Conduct review of published literature.

Develop list of variables and project plan.

Develop standard topic guide and information request for all participants.

Develop 12 structured, web-based data collection instruments for recording quantitative and qualitative feedback.

Review, organize, synthesize, analyze information; conduct 'reality checks.'

The two research investigators conducted a field test of the interview questions at four associations that had representation on the task force. Feedback from these test experiences led to revisions in the structured interview process.

Armed with data-gathering instruments, including checklists and lists of questions, the research investigators conducted on-site interviews at the nine organizations in the study group and the nine organizations in the comparison group. In all cases, they spoke with the CEO; other interviewees typically included senior and support staff representing a range of tenure at the association. These interviews were transcribed and attached to the detailed report prepared for each of the 18 associations.

In addition, each participating organization submitted, on average, three large boxes of documents—financial statements, 990 forms, annual reports, examples of products, publications, marketing plans, results of membership surveys, minutes of board meetings, and so forth. The research investigators used the financial data to generate charts and graphs that provided a historical perspective of net revenue, net profitability, ratio of net assets to total expenses, membership attrition, and level of reserves.

Once this data-gathering process concluded, the material needed to be reviewed through the eyes of association professionals. At this point, two task force members were assigned to each matched pair and given the task of studying the financial data, written reports, interview transcripts, and all the materials submitted by the associations. The two task force members in each pairing became, in essence, experts on their two assigned groups. Each of these teams made at least one visit to ASAE's headquarters, where the submitted materials were kept to maintain confidentiality. (All members of the task force and others involved in the research process signed confidentiality agreements.)

To guide the evaluation teams through the massive amounts of information collected, Collins offered a framework for analysis. He posed three questions that became the basis of each team's approach to formulating conclusions about the data:

- What did you find that ran counter to conventional wisdom?

- What did all the organizations have in common? In other words, what are the necessities for any organization to be considered good?

- What major factors accounted for the differences between the study and comparison groups?

After compiling an extensive list of conventional wisdoms related to association management (see Appendix D) and discussing the other two questions, the task force realized some necessary information was still missing. One representative from each team agreed to conduct a follow-up, on-site visit, including an interview with each CEO, to fill in the gaps and to get a better feel for each organization's culture and physical setting. A structured set of interview questions was developed to ensure that each team member asked the same questions, in the same order.

After completing the supplemental data collection, each team member wrote an individual dossier that analyzed the similarities and differences between the two groups. Next, the two members of each team pooled their thoughts and prepared one team dossier for distribution to the other task force members.

In January 2006, the task force convened to review all nine dossiers. This book presents the results of the discussions and debates that the task force engaged in to identify commonalities and differences across the groups and to put conventional wisdoms to the test.

Probability Versus Proof

Contrary to popular opinion, science does not deal with proof. Rather, it deals with prediction. The purpose of scientific research is to explain relationships and then predict the outcome of future events based on observation of the data.

Rarely can you say with certainty that one particular event or action causes a particular outcome. Usually, an outcome is caused by a combination of several variables acting together. Understanding the relationship among the variables enables you to predict outcomes.

For example, some critics have noted that research has never proven that smoking causes cancer. It takes only one exception to the hypothesis to disprove it: one smoker who never develops cancer.

But researchers have demonstrated that people who smoke are more likely to develop cancer than those who do not smoke.

Moreover, people with a family history of cancer have a greater likelihood of developing the disease, compared to those without that history. When these two factors—family history and smoking—are combined, the chances of developing cancer increase even more. You can predict, with a higher level of confidence, the likelihood of cancer.

The Measures of Success Task Force wanted to identify the factors remarkable organizations had in common, as distinct from the comparison group. To what degree any of these caused an association to be remarkable was outside the scope of the study. But by identifying the measures related to remarkable organizations, we could developed a means for predicting the likelihood that other organizations which possess the same attributes may also become remarkable.

To identify predictors of remarkable associations, we used a 2×2 analysis table. Suppose, for example, you wanted to determine if eye color is related to hair color. If you have 10 people with blond hair and 10 with brown hair, the 2×2 analysis table might look like this:

		Hair Color	
		# with brown hair	# with blond hair
Have brown eyes?	Yes	5	5
	No	5	5

By pure chance alone, you'd expect that each cell would contain five individuals. In that case, you'd conclude that there is no relationship between the color of hair and the color of eyes. If, however, the majority of brown-haired people have brown eyes and the majority of blond-haired people do not, you'd conclude that there *is* a relationship between hair color and eye color.

We used the same logic to determine which factors, if any, were related to remarkable associations. For each measure—for example, a customer service culture—we asked if it were observed in both the study and the comparison groups. Based on pure chance, you'd expect that half of the organizations in both groups would exhibit a certain factor and half would not. In such a case, there would be no relationship between a certain measure and remarkable associations. If, however, the distribution was greater than expected by chance, it would point to a relationship.

Measures observed in at least six or more of the study group and *not* observed in fewer than six in the comparison group were determined to be characteristics of the remarkable group but not characteristics of the comparison group. To meet our criterion, the 2×2 table for any measure had to appear, at a minimum, like the sample below.

Measure: Customer Service Culture

		# of Study Organizations	# of Comparison Organizations
Demonstrated a customer service culture?	Yes	6	4
	No	4	6

This logic formed the basis for the identification of research results. Any factor displayed by a majority of the study group, but not displayed by a majority of the comparison group, was selected. It is also important to note that several variables may exist beyond those we identified. Nevertheless, these seven measures of success are unique among the study group and, therefore, are associated with remarkable associations.

In all cases, the team dossiers confirmed that all 18 organizations had been placed in the appropriate group, whether study or comparison. For all nine pairings, the associations in the study group outperformed their counterparts in the comparison group in a majority of areas. That's not to say there weren't bright spots among the comparison group; in fact, in several instances, those associations performed almost as well as their counterparts in the study group.

The task force's discussions uncovered both positive and negative correlations within and among the study and comparison groups. Again and again, the task force revisited these correlations, some of which withstood repeated scrutiny. Others did not, either because they were not present in a majority of the pairings or because the evidence was not overwhelming enough to substantiate them. Likewise, some conventional wisdom held true for the groups studied; other commonly held beliefs appeared to have shaky foundations.

More clarity emerged each time task force members asked, "What factors are most likely to lead to an association being remarkable?" In the end, they made judgment calls based on financial data, interviews, site visits, reviews of materials, and their own experiences as association executives.

Research Timeline

February 2002   Jim Collins, coauthor of *Built to Last* and author of *Good to Great,* speaks at DigitalNow conference.

August 2002   Members of Research Committee of The Center for Association Leadership meet with Collins to discuss the possibility of applying his research methodology to a multi-year research project involving associations. Collins agrees to provide guidance and serve as mentor during the project.

November 2002   Research Committee submits a proposal to the board of The Center for Association Leadership requesting funding for the Measures of Success project.

January 2003   After receiving approval to pursue the project, Research Committee forms Measures of Success Task

Force and names Michael E. Gallery, Ph.D., CAE, as chairman.

February– June 2003

Random (nth name) sample of 1,000 members of ASAE (CEOs, number-two executives, and industry leaders) invited to participate in the jurying process. They receive a request to nominate five associations that are viewed as "benchmark" organizations, have persisted against difficult circumstances, and enjoy active and engaged members. Survey garners 324 responses—a 32 percent response rate at the 95 percent confidence level—and generates list of 506 associations. A natural break in the rankings produces a list of 104 top vote-getters.

August 2003

Collins meets with task force to provide guidance on selection criteria for study and comparison associations.

September 2003

Two recent college graduates hired as research investigators to work full time on the project.

October 2003

Letters sent to top 104 associations identified through the jurying process, inviting them to participate and requesting preliminary membership and financial data.

November 2003

Follow-up letters sent to associations that had not yet responded.

December 2003

Overall, 55 associations respond (53 percent response rate), with 47 indicating a willingness to participate and eight opting to withdraw from consideration. Three other associations are eliminated because of tax status, age (less than 20 years old), and status as an allied society.

January 2004

From the remaining pool of 36 associations, the task force selects 22 as meeting its criteria for financial and membership health (more years in the black than in the red and growth or consistent maintenance of membership/market share numbers). The other 14 associations are excused from the study.

February 2004 Task force members personally contact the CEOs of seven associations that did not respond to the invitation to participate. Research investigators begin collecting 15 years of financial and membership data for associations that have agreed to participate and signed the Institutional Agreement.

March 2004 Task force members define 11 areas to study for each association and develop a series of questions for research investigators to ask during on-site visits. They also develop nine research pairings, matching each association in the study group with one in the comparison group. To keep the focus on aggregate results rather than one-on-one pairings, the task force decides not to publicly acknowledge which associations form the comparison group.

May 2004 Development of research instruments and interview questions to guide data collection in the 11 areas.

July– September 2004 Research team field tests and finalizes research instruments and interview questions at four beta-tested associations.

October 2004 Research investigators begin site visits to associations in both the study and comparison groups.

December 2004 Task force meets with Collins, who reviews his research methodology and outlines a process for analyzing the data.

March–May 2005 With majority of site visits and interviews completed, research investigators begin compiling detailed reports and analyses of data.

June–August 2005	Two task force members assigned to each research pairing; these teams review researchers' reports and interview transcripts as well as materials submitted by participating associations.
September 2005	Task force meets with Collins to share preliminary results of data analysis, identify gaps in information, and finalize remaining steps.
October–November 2005	Task force members conduct on-site visits to associations in both the study and comparison groups and interview CEOs to answer follow-up questions. Research investigators complete data collection and analysis.
December 2005	Based on research reports, interviews, on-site visits, and the materials review, each team member compiles an individual dossier on one pairing of control and comparison organizations.
January 2006	Drawing on their individual dossiers, members of each team compile a team dossier to share with other task force members. Measures of Success Task Force conducts its final meeting to analyze results of matched pairings and generate conclusions.

Research Tools

Complete List of Documents Requested

DOCUMENT	DESCRIPTION
ABOUT THE VISION	
Vision statement	Statement of vision for the organization
Value statement	Statement of value for the organization
Mission statement	Statement of mission for the organization
Purpose statement	Statement of purpose for the organization
Goal statements	Statement of goals for the organization
Transcripts of speeches	Transcribed speeches from CEO/ED or President/President-Elect
Transcripts of public addresses	Transcribed speeches from CEO/ED or President/President-Elect
MARKETS, COMPETITORS, AND THE ENVIRONMENT	
Staff allocated to market research	Number of staff assigned to market research
Budget allocated to market research	Budget dollars assigned to market research
Industry studies	Studies and reports on the industry, conducted by the organization
Market research utilization	Internal documents regarding how industry-related research is used
Membership studies	Studies and reports on the membership/donors, conducted by the organization
Membership surveys	Surveys conducted specifically within the membership

DOCUMENT	DESCRIPTION
Markets, Competitors, and the Environment, *continued* Membership research	Internal research done on the membership or member metrics
Membership research utilization	Internal documents regarding use of membership-related research
Member dues	Member dues from 1988–2003
Records of mergers within membership	Documentation of mergers affecting the membership
Recruitment efforts	Plans and programs used to recruit and retain members
Membership services to nonmembers	Summary of services offered to nonmembers; is there a difference in how the service is offered?
Environmental scans	Environmental scans conducted on factors affecting the organization
Benchmarking data	Data and metrics used by the organization
Questionnaires and surveys	Research tools used to assess attitudes or needs of membership or staff
Circulation of magazine	Number of people receiving the organization's magazine (1988–2003)
Core competencies for members	Defined core competencies for membership, if applicable
Member satisfaction studies	Studies pertaining to member satisfaction
Member demographics	Analysis of membership by age, gender, tenure, education, etc.
Staff allocated to marketing	Number of staff assigned to marketing functions
Budget allocated to marketing	Budget dollars assigned to marketing functions
Marketing plans	Marketing plans used internally by the organization

DOCUMENT	DESCRIPTION
Markets, Competitors, and the Environment, *continued* Member/donor retention goals	Measurable goals for member/donor retention
Member/donor retention performance	Realistic performance as compared to goals for member/donor retention
Member/donor acquisition goals	Measurable goals for total member/donor growth
Member/donor acquisition performance	Realistic performance as compared to goals for member/donor growth
Enrollment numbers	Total membership (1988–2003)
Membership numbers	Membership number broken down by category (1988–2003)
Long-term marketing plans	Internal longer-term marketing plans used by the organization
Marketing initiatives	Programs used for marketing to members
Marketing strategies	Strategies and planning for marketing products and services to members
Marketing implementation	Internal documents regarding how members were marketed to
Media kits	Promotional materials for annual meeting, magazine, and journal advertising
ORGANIZATIONAL ARRANGEMENTS	
Organizational chart that includes board, staff, and volunteers	Graphic representation of volunteer-to-staff relationship
Bylaws and historical amendments	Organization bylaws and amendments made (1988–2003)
Articles of Incorporation	Articles of Incorporation for the organization
Outsourced functions	List of functions outsourced by the organization

DOCUMENT	DESCRIPTION
Organizational Arrangements, *continued* Consultants used	List of consultants the organization has used
Job descriptions	Description of all staff positions in the organization
National officers	List of board members in the organization (1988–2003)
National staff	List of employees (1988–2003)
USE OF TECHNOLOGY	
Technology staff	Number, qualifications, and salaries of staff assigned to organization's technology functions
Technology budget	Annual budget dollars assigned to technology
Hardware expenditures	Annual expenditures on hardware (1988–2003)
Software expenditures	Annual expenditures on software (1988–2003)
Tech support expenditures	Annual expenditures on tech support (1988–2003)
Technologies employed	List of all technologies used internally
Technological advances	Highlights of major technology advances within the organization (1988–2003)
BUSINESS STRATEGY/STRATEGIC PROCESS	
Published information on strategic plans	Strategic and operational plans
Published information on strategic planning process	Internal documentation of planning process
Meeting minutes	Internal staff meeting minutes
Crisis management documents	Planning for and documentation of crisis management policies

DOCUMENT	DESCRIPTION
Business Strategy/Strategic Process, *continued* Strategic partnerships	List of alliances or collaborations entered into by the organization
PRODUCTS AND SERVICES	
Major vendor services	List of major vendors used by the organization
Conference revenue	Annual conference revenue (1988–2003)
Conference expenses	Annual conference expenses (1988–2003)
Member awards programs	List of award programs for members
Magazine distribution	Numbers and demographics of magazine readers (1988–2003)
Journal distribution	Numbers and demographics of journal readers (1988–2003)
Certification materials	Materials pertaining to certifications awarded by the organization
Program design	Documents on how programs move from conceptualization to implementation
Program development	Documents discussing how new programs are identified, developed, and implemented
Current products and services	List of products and services offered by organization
Sales history	Revenue generated from sales of goods (1988–2003)
Market research for products	Documents pertaining to market research on specific products
Annual meeting schedules	Summary of how attendees spend their time at an annual meeting

DOCUMENT	DESCRIPTION
LEADERSHIP	
Board members, terms, and roles	List of board members (1988–2003) and their term definitions and responsibilities
Board policies and procedures	Policies and procedures manuals for board members
Standing committees	List of committees for the organization, including purpose and membership
Ad hoc committees	List of ad hoc committees and task forces, including purpose and membership
Board evaluations	Evaluation documents for board members
Role of staff	Documentation of role staff plays in board meetings and implementation of board decisions
Meeting minutes	Minutes from board meetings (1988–2003)
CEO contract	Contract of the current CEO
Board of Directors bylaws	Bylaws for the board and changes (1988–2003)
Volunteer recognition	Documents pertaining to awards and recognition for volunteer leaders
Board of Directors self-assessment	Self-assessment documents used by board members
Board orientation	Materials used for board orientation program
COMMUNITY AND CULTURE	
Staff demographics	List of employees by tenure, age, race, gender, education, title, and grade
Staff size	Number of employees (1988–2003)

DOCUMENT	DESCRIPTION
Community and Culture, *continued* Policies and procedures manual	Staff policies and procedures manuals (1988–2003)
History of lawsuits	Documentation of recorded lawsuits involving the organization
Succession planning	Defined succession planning documents
Training events and programs	List of events and programs for staff's professional development
History of staff restructuring and layoffs	Documentation of internal staff restructuring and layoffs
Performance appraisals	Performance appraisal documents for staff (blank or without names)
Benefits plans	Employee benefits
Exit reviews	Employee exit reviews (blank or without names)
Internal awards	Criteria pertaining to staff awards and lists of winners
External awards	Criteria pertaining to member awards programs and lists of winners
Code of ethics	Code of ethics for the organization, including changes (1988–2003)
Code of ethics enforcement	Documentation detailing enforcement of organization's code of ethics
Diversity	Documentation and materials regarding diversity programs and initiatives within the organization
FINANCIAL INFORMATION	
Statement of Financial Position	Statement of Financial Position (1988–2003)
Balance Sheets	Balance Sheets (1988–2003)
Statement of Cash Flows	Statement of Cash Flows (1988–2003)

DOCUMENT	DESCRIPTION
Financial Information, *continued* Budgets	Annual budgets (1988–2003)
Form 990	Form 990s (1988–2003)
Annual reports	Annual reports (1988–2003)
Non-dues revenue	Sources of non-dues revenue (1988–2003)
Donations and grants	Documentation of donations and grants to the organization
Investment policies	Documented investment policies for the organization
Fundraising	Documents outlining organization's fundraising initiatives
Liability insurance	Liability policies for the organization
Request for exemption	Request for exemption form
Reserve policy	Documented reserve policies for the organization
Financial audits	External audits of financial disclosures (1988–2003)
PUBLIC POLICY	
Amicus Curiae briefs	Amicus Curiae briefs presented by the organization
PAC bylaws	Bylaws of the organization's political action committee, if applicable
PAC financial disclosures	PAC treasurer notes, receipts, and expenditures, if applicable
Other PAC information	Additional documents related to PAC (e.g., committee meeting minutes)
OTHER DOCUMENTS COLLECTED	
Chapters	Number of chapters (1988–2003)
Member benefits	List of benefits received by members

DOCUMENT	DESCRIPTION
Other Documents Collected, *continued* Awards received	Documentation of any awards received by the organization
Membership application	Materials provided to prospective members
Constitution	Constitution for the organization, if applicable
Executive Committee	List of Executive Committee members (1988–2003)
Policy statements	Policy or position statements issued by the organization

On-Site Interview Questions

The following structured set of interview questions was developed to ensure consistency. The research investigators spoke with the CEO and other senior and support staff representing a range of tenure at the association. These interviews were transcribed and attached to the detailed report prepared for each of the 18 associations.

Vision, Mission, and Purpose

How would you characterize the basic reason for this organization's existence? Has it changed over time?

Describe a difficult choice or important decision you have had to make. Did the vision, values, mission, or goals come into play in your decision or choice?

Markets, Competitors, and the Environment

Tell me about your markets (members and suppliers). Has the composition of either group changed over time? How has your organization adjusted to these changes?

How do your members and suppliers contribute to the success of your organization?

Who are your chief competitors? What do you view as their main competitive strengths and weaknesses, compared to this organization?

Do you perform formal scanning or market research? If you do conduct research, can you give me an example of how it was used?

Organizing Arrangements

Describe the relationships among the board, the CEO, and the staff. Has the structure, size, or style of governance changed since you came into this organization in your current capacity? Are there any new types of structures?

Have staffing levels and/or structure changed over the past 15 years?

How are board members and officers chosen? How is the CEO chosen?

Use of Technology

What have been the most important technological "events" to affect your organization during the past 15 years?

What has been your association's traditional approach to technology expenditures? Describe any major technology initiatives since you've been here.

Of which technologies does your organization make the greatest use?

Describe your organization's attitude toward technology: "early adopter," "early majority," "late majority," or "laggard"? Your members' attitude?

Business Strategy/Strategic Process

Over the past 15 years, can you describe two instances where the organization was forced by external events to cope with major change?

How did you define success? By that definition, was the change successful? Did you conduct any formal evaluation or measurement to assess the results?

Can you describe two examples where the organization initiated such change on its own? If so, why did you decide to undertake the change? How did you define success? By that definition, was the change successful? Did you conduct any formal evaluation or measurement to assess the results?

Looking back, is there anything that you wish you, or your organization, had done differently? Is there anything you are particularly proud of?

Products and Services

Describe the organization's "signature" products or services. Can you explain the development process and who was involved?

What, if any, role do members have in the product development process? What about board, staff, and suppliers?

Have you had any product failures? If so, what did you learn from the experience?

Have you engaged in any joint ventures or strategic alliances with other groups? If so, what prompted your decision to do so? What has worked well, and what hasn't?

Leadership

For the CEO:

What characteristics would you use to describe yourself and your leadership style? What do you consider to be your strengths and weaknesses?

Could you describe the process by which you were selected to lead this organization? Who made the ultimate decision, and who participated? What was it like—that is, how was it the same as previous experiences, and how was it different?

How do people move up in this organization? Is there a formal succession plan?

For Other Staff:

Which among the current CEO's qualities, skills, or experience were most appealing to the selection team? What were your feelings on this decision?

In terms of the leadership model/style here, what do you like and what do you dislike?

How do people move up in this organization? Is there a formal succession plan?

How would you describe the relationship between your CEO or leaders and the board? What works well? What doesn't? Why?

Culture and Community

What advice would you give to a new employee or volunteer about how to be successful in this organization?

Thinking about your job, what are you most excited about? Most worried about? Why?

Based on what you have told them, how do you imagine your friends or family would describe this association as an employer?

How much contact do you have with members on a daily basis? What is the nature and tone of the interaction?

Financial Issues

Over the past 15 years, how has your organization's financial situation changed? What internal or external forces influenced these changes?

What event in the past 15 years has affected your financial direction? Was this event anticipated, or was it a shock? How long were its effects felt? Were any countermeasures taken as a result? What was learned from this experience?

How do you determine capital and operational expenditures?

Explain the involvement of staff and volunteers in the financial management process.

How do you evaluate and report the impact of economic and budget factors on financial planning, investment policies, and financial performance?

How do you set and manage your reserve policy?

Physical Setting and Location

How, when, and by whom was your association's main office selected?

Is either the setting or the location of your organization's main office important to its mission?

Does the internal layout reflect any particular value or philosophy held by your association? Does it contradict any value or philosophy?

Public Policy

When an issue impacts your membership, what actions are taken and how quickly? Who makes the call on how and when to move forward with major decisions?

How involved are members in your PAC? How are contributions primarily allocated?

How does your membership support the public policy initiatives of the organization? Do the members make an impact on public policy initiatives?

Who identifies the public policy initiatives of the organization?

How do you determine the need for grassroots activities? How are they implemented and evaluated?

Follow-up Interview Questions for CEOs

A follow-up, on-site visit was conducted to gather more information, including getting a better feel for each organization's environment, such as its culture and physical setting. This visit included an interview with each organization's CEO. The following structured set of interview questions was developed to ensure consistency.

1. Please describe the relationship between strategic planning and budgeting in your association.
   - How involved are your members in driving change?
   - How are priorities set? Do you believe that priorities change as elected leaders change?
   - How is the strategic plan communicated throughout the organization to ensure its implementation?
   - How do you integrate the strategic plan into day-to-day operations?
   - How do you evaluate the outcomes of the strategic plan?
   - Has your planning/budgeting process changed within the last 5 to 10 years? If so, how?

2. What steps do you take to ensure you have the right people on your staff to carry out the strategic plan?

3. Please provide two or three examples of how implementation of the strategic plan has led to change in your organization.

4. Looking back over the last 10 years, what factors have contributed to your organization's success? What factors have impeded its success?

5. When you became the CEO, what were the top three changes you wanted to make? Why? What level of success did you achieve with those changes?

6. How does the board evaluate your success as the CEO?

7. Explain the process your association uses to identify, pursue, and finalize strategic alliances and other partnerships.

8. How does your association create and nurture future leaders within the membership?

9. At the end of the day, how do you measure the success of your organization?

Team Dossier

After completing the supplemental data collection, each task force team compiled a dossier that analyzed the similarities and differences between one matched pair (one study association and one comparison association). The entire task force reviewed all nine team dossiers as the starting point for generating its findings.

Study Organization: _____

Comparison Organization: _____

1. What are the obvious differences between the two organizations?

2. What are the similarities between the two organizations?

3. In both organizations, what developments, occurrences, activities, etc., call into question the prevailing "conventional wisdom" within the association management field?

4. Share the details of at least one success story from the study group; if possible, contrast it with a similar situation at the comparison group that did not have as positive an outcome.

5. What is the essence of this particular pairing? In other words, "Why is one gold and the other silver or bronze?"

D

Frequently Asked Questions

1. What relevance does Jim Collins' research, conducted in the for-profit sector, have to voluntary associations?

Although many have studied the sources of excellence in for-profit organizations, few have addressed the definition—let alone the sources—of success in voluntary membership associations. A number of reasons for this informational deficit come to mind.

First, publicly traded companies are legally required to submit detailed financial reports to the Securities & Exchange Commission (SEC) on a quarterly basis. Additionally, the stock market (stock price) and the marketplace (sales volume, gross and net income, sources of revenue, and so forth) provide standardized measures of corporate performance. Because the SEC has standardized reporting requirements in terms of scope, content, types of information, unit of analysis (by corporation, by division, by geography), you can make apples-to-apples comparisons among various companies.

In contrast, most associations have a combination of 501(c)(6), 501(c)(3), and privately held, for-profit divisions housed under one umbrella. Requirements for reporting to the government are typically less frequent and less detailed. The true financial status of an association may also be more difficult to discern, because the umbrella organization may comprise several smaller organizations, each with a different legal structure and tax status. The diverse legal structures and inconsistent reporting requirements make it much more difficult to objectively assess or compare different associations' performances.

While solvency ensures an association's survival, making a profit is not its primary reason for existence. By their very nature, associations are mission-driven organizations whose fundamental *raisons d'être* are conceptual and intangible—and, therefore, difficult to quantify. Even if their tax status didn't prohibit associations from explicit pursuit of profits, their own goals would.

Finally, rigorous, quantifiable research is expensive to conduct. Whereas for-profit businesses have comparatively large research budgets, associations have less money to spend on this sort of activity.

2. How was the research team of association executives selected?

Members of the Measures of Success Task Force were selected based on their experience, plus the scope, size, and type of their employing organization. Having a broad cross-section of association executives and strategists was important to helping us stay unbiased and objective. Because the study included varying types of organizations, we sought varying expertise to help us understand and analyze the data from different perspectives.

3. What were your initial selection criteria for the associations in the study group?

Candidates for the study group needed to have:

- Been in operation for at least 20 years;
- Finished more years in the black than in the red;
- Exhibited the ability to retain members, donors, or market share during the study period; and
- Had more than one CEO during the study period.

4. Why didn't you consider organizations that had one CEO for more than 15 years?

We attempted to follow as closely as possible the methodology that Jim Collins and Jerry Porras used in *Built to Last.* Like them, we were interested in identifying which factors contributed to an organization's greatness. We were looking for factors that were a part of the organization's fundamental structure and not a function of a specific product, service, or person.

For this reason, Collins and Porras elected to study companies founded before 1950. They argued that this time period would be sufficient to ensure a variety of products, services, and CEOs. Given the average age of associations, as well as the length of time that associations maintain records, we believed that a 15-year period would best serve our needs.

5. How did you accommodate inconsistencies in reporting and collecting data from the associations over 15 years?

The quality and quantity of the information submitted varied across organizations. For the 15-year period being studied, some associations simply didn't have electronic records of materials. Some did not have document retention policies requiring them to save the information, while others had insufficient documentation to correlate with their matched-pair counterparts.

Some organizations—such as AARP, Girl Scouts of the USA, and the Society for Human Resource Management—provided more information than we could possibly analyze in a couple of sittings. In an isolated case, one organization provided minimal information. Our research investigators put their curiosity to work and searched for information through secondary sources. We attempted to locate the exact same information about each organization. In some cases, that simply wasn't possible.

No organization provided the entire 15 years of information exactly as requested. We are confident that the information received supports the concepts in this publication.

6. Why are there so few trade associations in the study?

We made every attempt to ensure that we had sufficient representation from trade, professional, and philanthropic organizations. Collins' work involved publicly traded companies. He had access to an abundance of public documents published by those companies, as well as a massive amount of literature published in the popular press about his subjects.

We, on the other hand, were dealing with associations. The information we needed to review was not in the public domain. Our only means of acquiring it was through the voluntary cooperation of the associations. We identified several potential trade associations; however, we succeeded in gaining the cooperation of a few. Given that concern, we asked several representatives of trade associations to review our findings.

7. What was the stock price equivalent for associations?

Collins used stock price only in *Good to Great*. In *Built to Last*, Collins and Porras used a jurying process to identify great companies. Among the list generated from this process, they selected companies that had been founded before 1950.

In *Good to Great*, Collins was interested in studying companies that had started out good and became great. What, he wondered, had they done differently compared to the companies that had remained good?

Unlike his first study, in which he used a jurying process to identify highly visionary companies, Collins realized that the *Good to Great* study required the use of objective measures. He and his research team analyzed the stock performance of Fortune 500 companies. Among those, he identified 11 companies that realized and maintained a dramatic increase in their stock price while other companies in their industry maintained a good increase in their stock prices.

Our study employed the *Built to Last* methodology. Like Collins and Porras, we used a jurying process to identify an initial list of candidate organizations. Then we narrowed that list on the basis of three criteria:

- Financial performance as evidenced by consistently ending the year in the black.
- Consistent member (or donor growth) and low member attrition.
- In existence for at least 15 years and had more than one CEO.

8. How did you identify the conventional wisdoms?

Conventional wisdoms were identified based on the common themes and issues that arose during the review process. The conventional wisdoms were further vetted at a research retreat, where we had an opportunity to write all the qualitative and quantitative information in aggregate to dispel myths that did not hold up against our research findings.

During one of their many meetings, members of the Measures of Success Task Force—all seasoned association executives and strategists—generated the following list of statements of conventional wisdom:

- One person should be at the top.
- Keep 50 percent of annual expenses in reserves.
- CEO should be an association professional.
- CEO should come from outside the organization rather than within.
- Don't get too far ahead of the membership
- Elections should reflect the democratic process.
- Elected leaders should move through the ranks.
- Small boards are better than big boards.
- Organizations should be more member-driven than staff-driven.
- Be innovative/on the cutting edge.
- Run the association like a corporation.

- Engage in consensus decision making.
- Participatory management is best.
- CEO should take a back seat to the elected leader.
- CEO is always right.
- Have a one-year term for elected leaders.
- Association activities require constituent buy-in.
- Radical times require radical change.
- Proactive change is better than reactive change.
- The board sets the policy; the staff implements it.
- Staff should not be involved in selection of leaders.
- CEO has no vote on the board.
- Have a strategic plan.
- A higher market share is better.

As part of its final meeting, the task force compared its findings against this list to determine which statements, if any, were not consistent with those findings. The results of that analysis appear in Chapter 5—Old Saws and Fresh Cuts.

APPENDIX E

How to Measure the Measures

How well does your association perform on the seven measures?

This is an easy question to ask but a hard one to answer. For example:

- Many of the qualities that exemplify remarkable associations are intangible. The breadth and depth of a customer service culture (Measure 1) cannot be accurately measured by counting the number of "We love our members" plaques on the wall. Anyone can put up a plaque. Member focus is both an attitude *and* a set of practices.

- Several of the measures are not mutually exclusive. The presence of dialogue and engagement (Measure 4) and the model of the association CEO as broker of ideas (Measure 5) both reflect an organizational culture that values candor, where people from all quarters may speak freely without fear of retribution and innovate without being seen as disrespecting authority.

- Several measures are innately subjective and inevitably influenced by one's role in the association. As an example, an association's product development team may perceive its efforts as being closely aligned with the mission (Measure 2), while those engaged in product marketing may see things quite differently.

Fortunately, none of these issues presents an insurmountable obstacle to an association willing to embark on an objective measurement program. Doing so first requires a commitment to:

- Invest the time, money, and effort required to do measurement properly.

- Communicate the results broadly and with candor.

- Foster change in the areas identified as problematic by the research. Asking for feedback and then ignoring or discounting the messages received can diminish your organization's credibility as well as its ability to gather honest feedback in the future.

Outlined below are several methods that you can use to ascertain how well your association is performing on each of the commitments and the criteria (measures) on which they are built. Some options are more ambitious; others offer smaller, less expensive methods for conducting measurements.

Commitment to Purpose

Measure 1: A Customer Service Culture

Both organizational policies and processes and unrehearsed interactions with individual members consistently express a "We're here to serve you" attitude.

Potential Measurement Methods

- Develop a program to measure and analyze compliments and complaints. This is a simple and relatively inexpensive method of finding out what makes members feel valued and what engenders dissatisfaction.

- Administer the survey in the *7 Measures of Success Implementation Guide and Assessment Tool.*

- Conduct focus groups, using an independent moderator, with front-line employees at your association. Include those who answer the phones, interact with members and/or volunteers at meetings, and so forth. Often, the people on the front lines know a great deal about members and the association's attitudes toward them. Typically, front-line employees are also willing to speak candidly.

Measure 2:
Alignment of Products and Services with Mission

The association's mission remains consistent, and the association's portfolio of products and services is congruent with its stated mission.

Potential Measurement Methods

- Identify the presence or absence of a written mission statement. Is there any evidence to suggest that the mission has played a meaningful role in shaping actions across time? Review minutes of meetings leading to and/or announcements of significant changes to see whether specific elements of the mission are mentioned.

- Look at major sources of income and areas of investment across a 10-year period. Do products and services that explicitly reflect the mission provide a major source of income? Has the association consistently invested time, money, and effort in the development of mission-consistent products and services?

- Conduct focus groups, using an independent moderator, organized around the topic: "What is our mission?" Hold focus groups with members, staff at all levels, and volunteers—but do not tell them in advance that you will be asking this question.

Commitment to Analysis and Feedback

Measure 3: Data-Driven Strategies

Remarkable associations have developed an expertise in gathering information as well as processes for sharing and analyzing the data to deduce what actions the data point to taking.

Potential Measurement Methods

- Count the number of channels through which you gather information, the types of information collected, and the places in your organization that engage in such activities. You may use informal channels, such as conversations with members or colleagues, and/or formal market research studies. You may seek both qualitative data (from focus groups, for example) and structured, quantitative data in the form of surveys; the data may be collected at numerous points throughout your organization, including human resources, member relations, customer service, and so forth. The more you find in each area, the better.

- Determine what happens to the information collected through the various methods. Does it ever move beyond the point of contact? To begin to tap its promise, information must be recorded, shared, and analyzed in relation to information from other sources.

- Next, ask "Does the information get communicated? If so, how is it communicated and to whom?" Information can be a powerful tool for framing and motivating action. Far from hurting your organization, transparency engenders trust, motivates change, and fosters innovation.

- Exercise discipline to collect accurate data. Specifically, record the information you collect in a standardized format and adhere to professional standards when conducting formal market research. Designing and administering a survey correctly requires skill and formal training; this responsibility should not be assigned to people who are not fully qualified. Remarkable associations believe in good, solid research and commit the resources necessary to do it well.

Measure 4: Dialogue and Engagement

An internal conversation continually occurs among staff and volunteers about the organization's direction and priorities.

Potential Measurement Methods

- Conduct an employee survey, using either a standardized or customized survey program, to learn about the state of communication within your association. Ideally, seek the advice of an independent expert who has advanced training in psychometrics and the particular quirks of employee survey management. (Hint: Confidentiality issues loom large in employee surveys.) This expert should not have any institutional ties that could bias his or her advice, such as being employed by a company that sells survey instruments.

- Use 360° assessments of randomly selected employees, volunteers, staff, members, and suppliers as another means of discerning the state of communication within your association. Again, many such instruments are available; ideally, seek the advice of an independent expert before making your selection.

Measure 5: CEO as Broker of Ideas

Although the CEO may be visionary, what's more important is that the CEO facilitates visionary thinking throughout the organization.

Potential Measurement Methods

- Review the tenure of current and past CEOs. Can you find examples of ideas, new products or services, or initiatives that were generated by someone else? If so, how many were there? Did any of these initiatives receive institutional support in the form of time, money, and/or publicity? If so, how did the level of support compare to initiatives that originated with the CEO? How many of these proposals were ultimately implemented?

- On a daily, weekly, or monthly basis, determine how much time the CEO spends—outside his or her office and/or the association's headquarters—listening to and interacting with various stakeholders. How much time does the CEO spend learning about the world beyond the borders of the association? How often does he or she present truly new material, in any forum, for review and discussion? A simple count of such events can be highly instructive.

Commitment to Action

Measure 6: Organizational Adaptability

Remarkable associations learn from and respond to change; although willing to change, they also know what not to change.

Potential Measurement Methods

Answering the following questions can help you assess your association's level of adaptability during times of change:

1. How does the association monitor and respond to future trends, threats, and opportunities likely to impact the association's environment?

2. How open have the association's leaders been in discussing changes that will likely affect the association's environment?

3. In addressing the change, did the association's leaders seek input from staff, members, volunteers, and/or the board? If so, from whom?

4. Has the association faced a financial dilemma, a sudden and dramatic loss in membership, or a serious public relations issue? If so, what—if any—lessons were learned? How did the situation affect the association's strategic decisions?

According to research by C.R. Wanberg and J.T. Banas reported in the *Journal of Applied Psychology* ("Predictors and Outcomes of Openness to Changes in a Reorganizing Workplace," February 2000), resilient organizations do the following in times of crisis:

- Acknowledge that positive and negative changes exist, while projecting realistic optimism.

- Provide information generously, to all concerned.

- Invite participation on the part of all stakeholders in learning from and adapting to change, while simultaneously lending social and personal support to all affected.

Thus, answers to the four questions above are proxy measures for adaptability; the questions should be posed to all stakeholders.

Measure 7: Alliance Building

Associations that are secure and confident in their own right seek partners and projects that complement their mission and purpose.

Potential Measurement Methods

Measuring your association's ability to build successful alliances goes beyond basic counting. Determine, for instance:

1. How many alliances has the association sought during the past 10 years? Why?

2. How many alliances have been formalized during that same time?

3. Who are the association's unconventional partners?

4. When seeking alliances, does the organization have a list of criteria describing the type of alliance it wishes to form and the nature of its relationship to the association's strengths, weaknesses, mission, vision, and/or goals?

5. With any alliance ultimately formed, did the association establish metrics for success in advance?

6. Has the association ever evaluated an alliance partner and ultimately declined to work together? Why?

The answers to these questions will help an association begin to assess the extent to which any alliances were considered in terms of their alignment with mission and goals, core competencies, and the association's willingness to invest in careful planning to enhance success.

Sir Francis Bacon noted that knowledge is power. Like any other powerful tool, the information embodied by the seven measures confers power on the user only if that information is collected carefully and ethically and used responsibly—in the service of the association's stakeholders and its goals.

F

Participating Organizations

ASAE gratefully acknowledges the following organizations for generously sharing data and information for consideration in this research study.

AARP
The Aluminum Association
American Academy of Family Physicians
American Automobile Association
American College of Cardiology
American College of Healthcare Executives
American College of Surgeons
American Dental Association
American Diabetes Association
American Petroleum Institute
American Psychological Association
American Society of Civil Engineers
American Speech-Language-Hearing Association
American Thyroid Association
American Veterinary Medical Association
Associated Builders and Contractors
Associated General Contractors of America
Association of Healthcare Philanthropy
Boys and Girls Club of America
California Association of Realtors

Conference of State Bank Supervisors
Council of Christian Colleges and Universities
Edison Electric Institute
Equipment Leasing Association
Florida Chamber of Commerce
Girl Scouts of the USA
Illinois Association of Realtors
International City/County Management Association
Meeting Professionals International
Michigan Association of Home Builders
National 4-H Council
National American Indian Housing Council
National Association of Chain Drug Stores
National Association of College Stores
National Association of Counties
National Association of Secondary School Principals
National Association of Social Workers
National Association of Wheat Growers
National Business Travel Association
National Collegiate Athletic Association
National Paint and Coating Association
National Restaurant Association
National Roofing Contractors Association
National School Boards Association
Ohio Society of Certified Public Accountants
Radiological Society of North America
Save the Children
Society for Human Resource Management
Southern Association of Orthodontists
Southland Regional Association of Realtors
United Way

Contributors

A S MEMBERS of ASAE & The Center for Association Leadership's Measures of Success Task Force, the following individuals contributed countless hours to reviewing data, preparing analyses and reports, and engaging in wide-ranging discussions. This book represents the culmination of their efforts during the course of several years.

James G. Dalton, president, Strategic Counsel, Derwood, Maryland

Phyllis L. Edans, CPA, CAE, chief financial officer, American College of Emergency Physicians, Irving, Texas

Michael E. Gallery, Ph.D., CAE, president and founder, OPIS, LLC, Highland Village, Texas (chair of the task force)

Mark J. Golden, CAE, executive director and chief executive officer, National Court Reporters Association, Vienna, Virginia

Richard B. Green, vice president of association sales, Marriott International, Inc., Washington, DC

Wayne H. Gross, CAE, Smyrna, Georgia

Pamela Hemann, CAE, president, Association Management Services, Inc., Pasadena, California

Wells B. Jones, CFRE, CAE, chief executive officer, Guide Dog Foundation for the Blind, Smithtown, New York

Sherry L. Keramidas, Ph.D., CAE, executive director, Regulatory Affairs Professionals Society, Rockville, Maryland

Hugh K. Lee, president, Fusion Productions, Webster, New York

Dawn M. Mancuso, CAE, MAM, executive director and chief executive officer, Association of Air Medical Services, Alexandria, Virginia

Michelle I. Mason, CAE, vice president of strategic research, The Center for Association Leadership, Washington, DC

David J. Noonan, deputy executive vice president, American Academy of Ophthalmology, San Francisco, California

Sandra R. Sabo, writer and editor, Sandra R. Sabo Editorial Services, Mendota Heights, Minnesota

Sarah J. Sanford, CAE, executive director, Society of Actuaries, Schaumburg, Illinois

Susan Sarfati, CAE, president and chief executive officer, The Center for Association Leadership, and executive vice president, ASAE, Washington, DC

Acknowledgments

T HIS BOOK represents the fruit of almost four years' labor. From
September 2002 through January 2006, under the diligent chair-
manship of Michael E. Gallery, Ph.D., CAE, members of the Measures
of Success Task Force reviewed mountains of documents, analyzed
spreadsheets, and engaged in numerous discussions about what the
data were really saying. Dr. Gallery's tireless leadership and vision
were instrumental in bringing this project to completion.

This effort offered the best learning opportunity of task force
members' professional careers. All appreciate ASAE & The Center
for Association Leadership's support of this important contribution
to the association community.

The task force's work would not have been possible without the
staff of ASAE & The Center for Association Leadership, notably
Michelle Mason. As vice president of research programs, she shep-
herded the Measures of Success project through all its stages, from
concept to execution, and ensured it remained on track no matter
what obstacles arose. She also served as the liaison to Jim Collins and
his organization.

Collins encouraged the task force and staff to bring "the curiosity
of chimps" to the project, which included several "chimposiums"—
meetings focused on exploring the intriguing questions raised by the
research. The groundwork for these meetings was laid by Elizabeth
Farner and Bradley Feuling. Hired by ASAE as much for their

curiosity as for their educational credentials, Farner and Feuling doggedly tracked down information by phone, via the internet, and in person; conducted interviews with a wide range of association personnel, from CEOs to receptionists; and produced pages upon pages of spreadsheet analyses. When both Farner and Fueling headed to graduate school, their successor, Anna Cruz, matched their talents and perseverance.

Before beginning on-site visits to the participating organizations, Farner and Fueling finalized the questions and honed their interviewing skills at four task force members' organizations. Most deserving of thanks for serving as "beta test sites"—although not included in the study—are the American Academy of Ophthalmology, American College of Emergency Physicians, Guide Dog Foundation for the Blind, and Regulatory Affairs Professionals Society.

To help task force members review and process the data amassed by staff, Sara Wedeman, Ph.D., founder of Behavioral Economics Consulting Group, LLC, developed online tools to aid the interviewing process and provided statistical analysis. Wedeman's familiarity with Collins' concepts, as well as her ability to succinctly summarize trends within the data, contributed to the success of the task force's final chimposium.

A special thank you goes to Sandy Sabo, freelance writer and editor, who converted a mixture of task force members' thoughts, observations, discussions, and conclusions into a cohesive manuscript.

We are also very grateful and would like to thank Elena Gerstmann, CAE, staff director at IEEE. As chair of the research committee, Elena reviewed the updated edition and provided helpful suggestions for a more polished final publication.

A final note of appreciation goes to all donors. Thanks to their generous financial support, we were able to undertake this comprehensive, ground-breaking research project that will have ramifications for many years to come.

Donors Acknowledgment

The Center for Association Leadership

THANKS TO generous donations from associations, industry partners, and individuals, ASAE: The Center for Association Leadership and the ASAE Foundation are able to conduct its strategic research agenda. We thank our numerous past and present donors who have pledged significant contributions to our research endowment. Through their charitable support of our strategic research, ASAE member associations are beneficiaries of cutting-edge resources that facilitate a stronger and more vibrant association community. Together, our members and industry partners are building a better tomorrow.

Please visit **www.asaecenter.org/foundation2/html/supporters** to see our donor lists.

Advancing Association and Nonprofit Leadership

ASAE Foundation's Strategic Research is transforming the future of associations. If you are interested in learning more, getting involved, or contributing, please email strategicresearch@asaecenter.org.

Index